Contents

HAITI
FAMILY
BUSINESS

Latin America Bureau

Special Brief

First published in Great Britain in 1985 by **Latin America Bureau** (Research and Action) Limited, 1 Amwell Street, London EC1R 1UL

British Library Cataloguing in Publication Data

Prince, Rod
    Haiti: family business.
    1. Haiti — History — 1934-
    I. Title   II. Latin America Bureau
    972.94'07   F1928

    ISBN 0-906156-19-X

Written by Rod Prince with additional material by Jean Jacques Honorat
Map by Michael Green © Latin America Bureau
Cover photo by Mark Edwards/Earthscan, inset courtesy of West India
    Committee, shows wedding of Jean Claude Duvalier and Michèle
    Bennett
Cover design by Jan Brown
Typeset, printed and bound by Russell Press Ltd, Nottingham
Trade distribution in UK by Third World Publications, 151 Stratford Road,
    Birmingham B11 1RD
Distribution in USA by Monthly Review Foundation

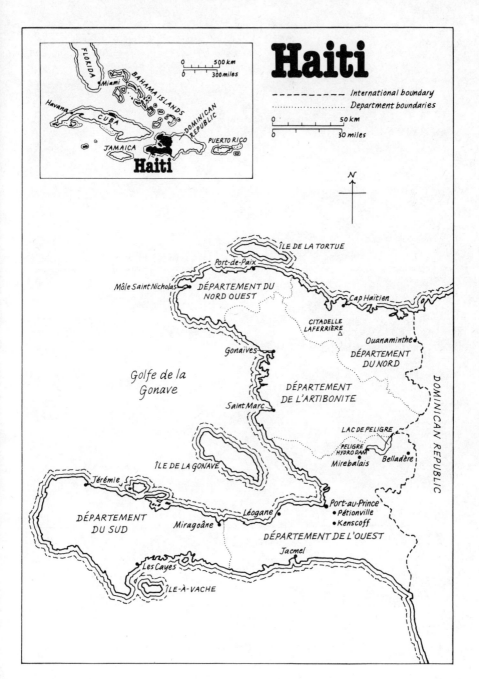

Haiti

FLORIDA

Miami

BAHAMA ISLANDS

Havana

CUBA

DOMINICAN REPUBLIC

JAMAICA

PUERTO RICO

Haiti

500 km
300 miles

– – – – – – – International boundary
················· Department boundaries

50 km
30 miles

N

ÎLE DE LA TORTUE

Port-de-Paix

Môle Saint Nicholas

DÉPARTEMENT DU
NORD OUEST

Cap Haïtien

CITADELLE
LAFERRIÈRE △

Ouanaminthe

DÉPARTEMENT
DU NORD

Gonaïves

Golfe de la
Gonave

DÉPARTEMENT
DE L'ARTIBONITE

Saint Marc

LAC DE PELIGRE

PELIGRE
HYDRO DAM

Belladère

Mirebalais

DOMINICAN REPUBLIC

ÎLE DE LA GONAVE

Jérémie

DÉPARTEMENT
DU SUD

Léogane

Miragoâne

Port-au-Prince
• Pétionville
• Kenscoff

DÉPARTEMENT DE L'OUEST

Jacmel

Les Cayes

ÎLE-À-VACHE

1 Haiti in Brief

Geographical position

Haiti covers the western third of the island known as Hispaniola, the second largest of the Caribbean islands. It is bounded on the same island by the Dominican Republic to the east; its nearest neighbours are Jamaica to the south-west and Cuba 50 miles to the north-west.

Area	27,750 sq km
Administrative divisions	9 departments, 119 communes, 555 rural districts
Land distribution (in hectares)	Cultivated land 916,750 (of which 687,560 is hill land and 229,190 flat land)
	Forests 200,000 (of which 75,000 is pine trees and 125,000 deciduous and others)
	Grazing land 500,000
	Non-productive land 1,071,000
	Other (rivers, lakes, roads, towns and villages) 30,000
	Offshore islands: La Gonâve, L'Ile-à-Vaches, Les Cayemites (Grande et Petite), La Navase, La Tortue

1

Population

Total	5.1 million (1982)
Growth rate	1.8% (1975-1980)
Urban	1.3 million (26%) 1982
Rural	3.8 million (74%) 1982
Density	absolute — 182 per sq km (1982)
	relative — 345 per exploitable sq km

Principal towns

Port-au-Prince (administrative and commercial capital)	766,000 inhabitants (1984)
Cap-Haitien	52,000 inhabitants (1982)
Les Cayes	38,000 inhabitants (1982)

Religion	Official — Roman Catholic
	Popular — Voodoo
Languages	Official language — French (spoken by 7-10%)
	National language — Creole (spoken by 100%)

Education	National	Urban	Rural
Population of school age	902,400	271,900	630,500
Percentage at school	27%	60%	14%
Primary education	23%	45%	14%
Secondary education	4%	15%	0
Vocational training	19% of secondary students		

Public expenditure on education (1984-85): US$3.70 per capita; 1.0% of GDP

Health

Inhabitants per doctor	8,200 (1984)
Hospital beds	3,868 (0.77 per 1,000)
Life expectancy	48 years (1982)
Infant mortality rate	124 per 1,000 (1977)

Public expenditure on health (1984-85): US$3.44 per capita; 0.9% of GDP

Nutritional situation: endemic malnutrition, chronic problems of undernourishment.

Military Budget	8.3% of GDP (1982)

2

Statistical and other information on the Haitian economy has been taken from documents produced by the World Bank, IMF, US Government, Inter-American Development Bank, UN agencies and similar bodies, as well as by the Haitian government. However, all statistics on the Haitian economy should be treated with caution, partly due to inaccuracies of compilation, partly because the 'subsistence' economy cannot easily be measured in conventional statistical terms.

The Economy

GDP total	1982 US$865 million	
Per capita	1970 US$90 million	
	1984 US$100 million	

Per capita growth		
	1981	− 5.2%
	1982	− 4.9%
	1983	− 3.1%
	1984	0.4%

Labour force		
	Agriculture	57%
	Manufacturing	5.7%
	Construction	0.9% (1980)

Real wages (industrial)		
	1979	− 8.8%
	1980	18.3%
	1981	2.0%
	1982	− 2.6%

Inflation (Sept.- Sept.)		
	1979	15.4%
	1980	15.3%
	1981	16.4%
	1982	6.2%
	1983	12.2%
	1984	8.6%

Trade

	US$million	
	Exports	Imports
1981	150	358
1982	174	336
1983	179	352
1984	200	350

Major exports	Coffee 21.6% US$51 million (1983) Bauxite 10.8% Free zone manufactures (baseballs, lingerie) 37.4% Other export crops: mangoes, essential oils, cocoa
Major trading partners	Exports to: US 59%, France 13%, Italy 7% Imports from: US 45%, Netherland Antilles 10%, Canada 8% (1980)

Foreign Debt
(public)

1981	US$372million
1982	US$410million
1983	US$446million
1984	US$600million

Debt per capita	1982	US$78

Debt service as
ratio of total
exports

1977	2.3%
1983	5.0%

Haiti occupies the western third of the island of Hispaniola, with the Dominican Republic taking up the eastern two-thirds. During the Spanish colonial period, the whole colony was known as Santo Domingo, after the city which remains the capital of the Dominican Republic.

When the western part was ceded to France by the Treaty of Ryswick in 1697, it took the name Saint-Domingue. When Jean-Jacques Dessalines declared independence on 1 January 1804, he named the country Haiti. This was the name, meaning 'land of mountains,' given to the island by its Taino indian inhabitants before the arrival of the Spanish.

During the nineteenth and early twentieth centuries, the name was commonly spelt Hayti, and this spelling has been followed here when quoting from documents of the time.

Chronology

1492	5 December — Christopher Columbus lands at the Môle St Nicholas.
1492-1503	The Amerindian population (Arawaks and Caribs) are enslaved by the Spaniards and decimated by work in the gold mines.
1520s	African slaves are first brought to Haiti.
1629	French pirates and buccaneers seize La Tortue and make it their base. They gain a foothold on the mainland, and move progressively into the interior.
1685	Publication of the Negro Code — a series of regulations inspired by Colbert which set out to organize the black slave trade and colonial methods of production.
1697	The treaty of Ryswick confirms France's sovereignty over the western part of Hispaniola island.
1749	Foundation of Port-au-Prince, capital of the French Windward Islands.
1770-1790	Saint-Domingue, known as La Petite France (Little France), or the Grande Isle à Sucre (the Great Sugar Island) accounts for two thirds of France's foreign trade. The population in 1791 is made up of 40,000 white settlers, 28,000 mulattoes and 450,000 black

5

slaves. Increasing numbers of maroons (slaves who escape to the mountains and live there free).

1791	General slave uprising.
1793	Slavery abolished in Saint-Domingue.
1795	Treaty of Bâle, under which Spain cedes the eastern part of the island to France. Spain recovers sovereignty in 1809.
1801	Toussaint L'Ouverture establishes the island's autonomy under French suzerainty.
1802-03	Napoleon Bonaparte sends a punitive expedition to restore colonial rule and reintroduce slavery. War of Independence. Toussaint captured and exiled in June 1802; dies in French prison, 27 April 1803.
1804	1 January. Jean-Jacques Dessalines proclaims independence. The country readopts its Indian name of Haiti (mountainous land).
1806	Dessalines assassinated.
1807-20	Henry Christophe rules north, from 1811 as King.
1807-18	Alexandre Pétion governs separate republic in south, Peasant uprisings in Grande Anse.
1820	Haiti reunified under Pétion's successor, Jean-Pierre Boyer.
1822-44	Haiti occupies Santo Domingo.
1825	Independence of Haiti recognized by France in exchange for huge indemnity.
1888-1915	Political instability and factional government increase.
1915-34	Occupation by US Marines.
1915-19	Resistance by peasant guerrillas led by Charlemagne Péralte.
1946, 1950, 1956	The army seizes power after outgoing presidents try to remain in office.
1957	François 'Papa Doc' Duvalier elected President.
1958	Civil militia known as the Tontons Macoutes or Volontaires de la Sécurité Nationale (VSN — National Security Volunteers) founded.
1964	Proclamation of the Presidency-for-Life.

1971   Duvalier dies. Proclamation of his 19-year-old son Jean-Claude as Haiti's ninth President-for-Life.

The Haitian cabinet

The composition of the cabinet in May 1985 was as follows:

Ministers of state

Presidency, information and public relations: Jean-Marie Chanoine
Interior and defence: Roger Lafontant
Finance and economy: Frantz Merceron
Justice: Théodore Achille

Ministers

Foreign affairs and worship: Jean-Robert Estimé
Labour and social affairs: Arnold Blain
Public works, transport and communications: Maxime Léon
Education: Gérard Dorcely
Agriculture, natural resources and rural development: Frantz
    Flambert
Planning: Yves Blanchard
Youth and sports: Serge Conille
Mines and energy: Franck Romain
Health and population: Victor Laroche
Trade: Jean-Michel Ligondé
Without Portfolio: Jules Blanchet

2 Introduction

Less than 200 years ago, the Haitian people launched a revolution which overthrew slavery and established the world's first independent black republic. In the course of the revolution, the Haitians defeated British, French and Spanish armies and shook the colonial slave empire throughout the Caribbean.

Haitians today live in conditions of appalling poverty and squalor under the Duvalier family dictatorship. The country is a byword of terror and corruption, living off hand-outs from overseas — principally from the United States. This Special Brief attempts to explain how this state of affairs came about, and how and why it is maintained.

Haiti: Family Business takes a necessary look at Haiti's past, but is mainly concerned with the modern Haitian economy, system of government, social structure and international relations.

Certain themes and patterns reappear throughout Haiti's history such as: the tradition of armed intervention in government, the absence of any developed political system and the long standing practice of presidents regarding state finance as their personal property. In this respect, Haiti is very much a 'family business' of whoever is the ruling elite of the time. It was this last feature which led a Canadian parliamentary committee in 1982 to describe Haiti as a 'kleptocracy' in which anything of value is liable to be appropriated by the ruling elite and their officials, at every level of the system.

These practices, however, are not a Haitian invention. They arose in the colonial state of Saint-Domingue and have thrived since then because of the circumstances in which the Haitian state came into being, and the conditions under which it has to survive.

Today, as for much of this century, the attitudes and policies of the United States are powerful factors influencing the course of events in Haiti; but the US does not control Haiti and does not always know what to do there. In nearly 30 years of the Duvalier family's rule, the US government has veered from support of the regime, through opposition (even including an attempt to bring Francois Duvalier down in 1963), back to acquiescence and eventually again to active support. Recent difficulties in the relationship may prove to be yet another passing phase, another tiff to be patched up in due course. There will always be tensions between Port-au-Prince and Washington as long as the Duvaliers insist on operating by their own rules, rather than accepting the position conventionally laid down for heads of client states in the US sphere of influence.

However, like the rest of the Caribbean, Haiti has seen increasingly strong pressure for change. The industrial development of the last fifteen years has led to rising discontent among those dispossessed or bypassed by it; witness the exodus of the boat people, the food riots and demonstrations of recent years. As Haiti is 'modernized' economically and bound more closely to the international financial system, so more Haitians are seeking a political opening and demanding the observance of constitutional and political rights. Arrest, brutality and imprisonment has so far been the regime's response. It could soon prove inadequate.

3 History

The Spanish settlement

An unknown number of Taino Arawak people inhabited the island of Hispaniola when Christopher Columbus and a band of Spanish gold-seekers landed in December 1492, on what is now Haiti's north coast. There may have been half a million or more Tainos at the time; within 50 years all but a handful of them were dead.

Although Haiti was the site of the first European landing in the Americas, the discovery of gold in eastern Hispaniola meant that Spanish colonial development was concentrated at that end of the island. The relative neglect of the western part made it possible for French buccaneers to establish themselves there in the seventeenth century, a position which led to the island being divided between the French and Spanish colonial powers and eventually into two separate countries; Haiti and the Dominican Republic.

When he arrived, Columbus described the Tainos as 'loveable, tractable, peaceable and praiseworthy.' The key word was tractable. The Spanish lost no time in enslaving the Tainos to work in the gold mines and supply food to the colonizers. Those who refused were subjected to the customary barbarities: whipping, cutting off of ears and noses, rape and killing. A tribute of gold was demanded of every adult Taino under a royal edict described by the priest Bartolomé de las Casas as 'irrational, impossible, intolerable and abominable.' Fugitives were hunted down by dogs, while those who submitted died of exhaustion and ill-treatment from their overseers. Influenza, smallpox and typhus decimated the remainder. By 1508 the Taino population was down to 60,000, and in 1548 there were fewer than 500 left.

In the 1520s it was decided to import slaves from Africa. By this time, however, the Spanish settlement had started to decline as the workable gold reserves became exhausted. The Spanish quest for gold led the *conquistadores* to colonize Mexico in 1521 and Peru in 1532, and Hispaniola became a neglected backwater. The colony fell prey to raids by the English and French, and in 1586 Santo Domingo underwent a month-long attack by British forces led by Sir Francis Drake, during which the city was sacked and looted.

The Spanish decline continued throughout the seventeenth century. By 1681 the population numbered 2,500 whites and 3,800 blacks, of whom 1,100 were slaves. These few inhabitants were engaged in agriculture, producing hides and ginger for trade. From the 1620s onwards, English and French buccaneers established a base in the Ile de la Tortue (Tortuga Island), off the north-west coast of Haiti. From there the French, who had emerged as the dominant group among the buccaneers, gradually took hold of the western part of Hispaniola, with the Spanish falling back to the south-eastern part of the island. By the end of the century France was well in control of what is now Haiti, a situation recognized in 1697 when Spain ceded the area to the French under the name Saint-Domingue.

Sugar and slavery

The French established an extremely lucrative colony based on slavery; producing coffee, indigo, cocoa, cotton and above all, sugar. In 1767 Saint-Domingue exported 72 million pounds of raw sugar and 51 million of white, plus 1 million pounds of indigo and 2 million of coffee. Coffee exports, which had amounted to 7 million pounds in 1755, had increased to some 68 million by 1789. The colony's exports to France were worth more than twice its imports from that country. The 800 sugar plantations in Saint-Domingue produced more than all the English Caribbean islands put together and the colony's overall trade is said to have outstripped that of the thirteen North American colonies, requiring the use of 700 ships to carry the vast volume of goods.

The labour of hundreds of thousands of slaves shipped from Africa was behind this wealth. From 2,000 in 1681, the number of slaves in Saint-Domingue increased to 117,000 in 1730 and to 480,000 in 1791. Since the number of slaves imported over the same period is estimated at 864,000, the figures provide ample evidence of the extremely high death rate. Some estimates have suggested that the equivalent of the entire number of slaves was replaced every twenty years.

The basis of the colonial economy, including relations between Saint-Domingue and France, was exploitation. Trade with France amounted to 95 per cent of the total and the system known as the

11

'Exclusive' laid down that all exports and imports were to be carried in French ships. Sugar and cocoa had to be shipped raw for refining in France or heavy duties were payable. No manufacturing industry was allowed in Saint-Domingue or other French colonies, so that all manufactured goods required in the colony had to be purchased from France. The system brought immense prosperity to French ports like Nantes, Dieppe, Bordeaux and Marseilles, as well as supplying the capital inflow on which French industry could develop. This colonial pattern of trade remains intact to the present day in the French 'overseas territories' of Guadeloupe, Martinique and Guyane.

Essentially, the French saw their colonial possessions purely as a source of wealth which they were not even concerned to develop through long-term investment. The economic system which reigned in Saint-Domingue was a predatory one based on an enslaved labour force and unequal trade relations. As such, it contained the seeds of multiple conflicts between French metropolitan and colonial interests, and between rich and poor whites, whites and mulattoes and owners and slaves in Saint-Domingue.

The *grands blancs* — the rich planters and merchants — enjoyed the profits and status derived from their possessions, but nevertheless held grievances against the French government which from time to time broke out into open protest. The Exclusive prevented them from trading as they wished and was a prime source of discontent, tempered only by the substantial amount of illicit trade they were able to carry on with the North American colonies. Generally, the *grands blancs* were excluded from the political position in the colony which they thought was theirs by right; the colonial government gave effective power to a military governor and a civilian *intendant* appointed in Paris.

Saint-Domingue, however, was not a settler society in the way that North America, Latin America or South Africa were. Many of the *grands blancs* were impoverished aristocrats whose dream was to return to France as soon as they had amassed sufficient money. Those who could afford it left their estates in the hands of overseers while they absented themselves in France. Similar ambitions, with even less chance of realization, were harboured by the *petits blancs* — small farmers, craftsmen, shopkeepers, low-ranking officials and an assortment of adventurers and refugees from the law.

In an even more equivocal position were the mulattoes or *gens de couleur*, the children of white planter fathers and black slave mothers who had been given their freedom. Their numbers rose from 500 in 1703 to 28,000 in 1791, against 40,000 whites and 450,000 slaves. Many *gens de couleur* became property and slave owners themselves, a situation permitted by Louis XIV's *Code Noir* of 1685. By the end of

12

the French regime, they controlled a third of the colony's plantations. In an effort to hold them in check, the white-dominated colonial council passed a series of measures in the 1760s and 1770s restricting their rights. Certain professions were closed to them and they were forbidden to intermarry with whites or to reside in France. They were also obliged to wear different clothes from whites, sit in different parts of churches and theatres, and observe a 9pm curfew.

If the mulattoes were subject to legal discrimination, the slaves were kept down by extreme and arbitrary terror which went far beyond the provisions of the *Code Noir*. The owners, living in perpetual fear of the more numerous slaves, invented the most atrocious tortures for real or imagined infractions. Saint-Domingue, it was said, was 'a mill for crushing negroes as much as for crushing sugar cane.'

The colony was thus a volcano of irreconcilable conflicts and racial hatreds. To keep the conflicts in check and ensure that the process of extracting wealth continued to function, a militarized and authoritarian state was developed, run by the Navy Ministry in France. Saint-Domingue was first and foremost a military outpost, on guard against attack from rival colonial powers. The towns were heavily fortified, and administered by a military officer. There was a standing army of up to 3,000 men, and a militia comprising all adult white males. This military apparatus was also required for internal security, frequently in action against groups of runaway slaves or maroons. One such example was in the 1750s headed by Makandal, who planned an unsuccessful mass poisoning of slave owners but was captured and burnt alive in 1758.

The military officers in charge of towns and districts were the undisputed rulers of the areas they controlled. The governor-general had an unbounded power which the planters' assembly found impossible to counterbalance, and the financial administrator had absolute control over taxes. This power reflected the absolutism of the French monarchy, aided by the distance of Saint-Domingue from the metropolis. The colonial administrators eagerly took advantage of the opportunity to turn their power to profit. Many of them were recruited from among disgraced officers, bankrupt nobles or merchants, despatched to Saint-Domingue by some highly placed protector to regain their wealth and return to France as soon as possible. They shamelessly held the island's inhabitants to ransom, exacting tributes far higher than the official taxes. The chief sources of their revenue were the sale of trading permits, land and decisions on property matters, and involvement in smuggling rackets so widespread that in 1789 alone, 30 million pounds of sugar and 25 million pounds of coffee bypassed the official channels.

These two features of the colonial system — authoritarian military power and extensive corruption — became so deeply entrenched in the colony that they survived throughout the following 200 years as permanent and essential features of Haitian life.

Road to revolution

The French revolution of 1789, which attacked the authoritarian royal power structure in the name of liberty and equality, blew apart the colonial state in Saint-Domingue. It gave contending groups the opportunity to assert their interests against those of their rivals, bringing the swift collapse of the arrangements which had hitherto maintained stability in the colony. It only remained for the slaves to deliver the death-blow.

The first collision was between the *grands blancs* and the *petits blancs*. The *grand blancs*, who gained control of the new Colonial Assembly by excluding the mulattoes and setting a property qualification which effectively excluded the *petits blancs*, saw a chance of consolidating their power in a self-governing Saint-Domingue. While favouring a nominal tie with France through allegiance to the King, they rejected the authority of the National Assembly in Paris, and sought an end to the Exclusive. Their ambitions were resisted by a combination of the colonial authorities and the *petits blancs*, who feared for their position in such a self-governing arrangement.

The *petit blancs* gained support from others who felt their interests would be better served by remaining with France: lawyers and merchants, whose wealth came from their association with French companies, and the mulattoes. The combination was strong enough to hold in check the 'Patriots,' as the *grands blancs* were calling themselves, and they reacted with ferocious attacks on the mulattoes. When the National Assembly in Paris passed a decree on 8 March 1790 (giving the vote to all persons over 25 who fulfilled certain property qualifications), the Colonial Assembly refused to include the mulattoes under its provisions, saying that they were not 'persons,' but members of a 'bastard and degenerate race.'

The consequence was the ill-organized and unsuccessful attempt at a mulatto revolt led by Vincent Ogé and Jean-Baptiste Chavannes. Defeated by the white troops, Ogé and his followers fled to Santo Domingo but were sent back by the Spanish governor. Ogé, his brother and Chavannes were tortured and executed, and 21 others hanged. When the news of the executions reached Paris, popular revulsion forced the reopening in the National Assembly of the

14

question of racial discrimination and slavery, but few of the Assembly representatives could bring themselves to put their declared principles into practice to the extent of ending slavery. In May 1791 they agreed a token measure giving full citizens' rights to about 400 mulattoes born of free parents, but even this resolution was rescinded three months later. Mulatto spokesmen in the debate had in fact indicated that they wanted civil rights so as to be able to stand on equal terms with the whites as upholders of slavery. Nevertheless, the May decree was greeted with rage by the Patriots, and mulattoes were lynched in an outbreak of racial hatred.

The events of 1790-91 had done nothing to resolve the mulattoes' ambiguous position in which they were at the same time discriminated against by the whites but privileged in relation to the slaves. The failure to resolve the contradiction lies at the root of conflicts which have continued throughout Haiti's history.

The slave revolt

During these two years of conflict whites and mulattoes alike had been recruiting slaves to strengthen the various factions. In August 1791 the slaves themselves showed their hand. Starting at a voodoo ceremony in the north of the country, the revolt spread with great speed. Within six weeks 1,200 coffee estates and 200 sugar plantations had been burned, while 1,000 whites and 10,000 slaves had been killed. Compared with previous slave revolts, this was remarkable both in its scale and in the evident degree of organization. The slaves, initially led by Boukman, had co-ordinated their plans and succeeded in keeping them secret, so that the plantation owners were caught by surprise.

Boukman was captured and beheaded in the early stages of the uprising. It was some time after this, but before the end of 1791, that Toussaint l'Ouverture joined the revolt, initially as a doctor, subsequently as military leader. Toussaint, who had learnt to read and write as a slave and had held the relatively privileged position of plantation steward, introduced guerrilla tactics into the slave army. In December he took command of the army, assuming the rank of Brigadier-General.

In the decade of war which followed, Toussaint proved not only an outstanding military leader but a negotiator and politician of great skill, making and breaking alliances and out-manoeuvring opponents almost to the end. Fighting in 1793 with the Spanish and French royalists, he changed sides in 1794 when the new Republic in France issued a decree abolishing slavery on 4 February. With Spain defeated,

Toussaint and the French allied to expel the British, who had invaded in 1793. In April 1796 Toussaint became Lieutenant Governor of a colonial state within the French empire and set about restoring agricultural production and economic prosperity. His plans did not involve changing the plantation basis of production, but replaced slavery with a system of contract labour enforced by a *gendarmerie*. The Exclusive was broken by the signing of trade agreements with Britain and the United States.

White planters who had fled the country were encouraged to return, but only a handful responded; many mulattoes, now known as *anciens libres*, had also left. A new class, to which Toussaint himself belonged — the *nouveaux libres*, or slaves freed in 1793, now aspired to estate ownership and other key positions. The power of Toussaint and this class, which included high-ranking members of the army, was consolidated in 1800 with the defeat of General André Rigaud, the southern mulatto leader, after a prolonged and vicious civil war. The same year saw Toussaint's forces occupy Santo Domingo to safeguard the country against external forces. Successive delegates from the French government had been expelled in 1797 and 1798, leaving no obstacles to Toussaint's assumption of supreme power.

Toussaint used his army, now 20,000 strong, to create an authoritarian state which, like the pre-revolutionary colonial state, was geared to resisting external and internal threats and to ensuring economic discipline. Each district was governed by an army general, who headed a team of military officers responsible for making sure that production was maintained on the plantations. When Toussaint's second-in-command, General Moyse, led a rebellion in the north in which white planters were killed so that their estates could be redistributed to landless ex-slaves, Toussaint had him shot without trial.

As well as perpetuating the tradition of the militarized state, Toussaint also carried forward another custom which has lasted to the present day: personal control of state finances. He alone managed the treasury and was unaccountable to any institution.

Toussaint was captured and exiled in 1802 by Napoleon's brother-in-law, General Charles Le Clerc, who had invaded with a mammoth expeditionary force. He died in April 1803, imprisoned in the French Jura. The French success was short-lived; national resistance led by Jean-Jacques Dessalines and Henry Christophe smashed the French armies, thousands of whose men had fallen victim to yellow fever. On 1 January 1804 Dessalines declared Haitian independence. His secretary is said to have commented on the occasion: 'We will write this act of independence using a white man's skull for an inkwell, his skin for parchment, blood for ink and a bayonet as pen.'

Independent Haiti

It was not until 1825 that Haitian independence was recognised by France, and even then only on extremely onerous terms. France required an indemnity of 150 million French francs, payable mainly to French planters who had lost their property in the revolution. The sum was reduced in 1838 to 60 million, but was nevertheless a burden which the devastated Haitian economy could only repay by borrowing from French, and later US, banks. The debt was not repaid until 1922.

At the same time, the plantation system was crumbling. It was Dessalines who first recognized that the large land holdings would have to be reorganized to satisfy the land hunger of the freed slaves, a realization which undoubtedly contributed to his assassination in 1806, since the plan would have harmed the interests of the mulatto landowners. After his death, Haiti split into a northern state ruled by President (later King) Henry Christophe, and a southern republic under the mulatto President Alexandre Pétion. In the latter, land was distributed to army officers and men and plots of various sizes were sold. This principally benefited mulattoes. Christophe later followed a similar policy, though here blacks also acquired large estates. The country was only reunified in 1820.

The plantation system had, in any case, become generally inoperable because the former slaves simply deserted the land and disappeared into districts where they could start their own smallholdings. One result was that landowners started renting their holdings out and retreating to the towns to further their careers as traders or officials. This movement primarily benefited the cities (especially Port-au-Prince), and began a tradition of absentee landlordism which still exists. Likewise, the ex-slaves' search for land led them to make forest clearings, starting a cycle of deforestation and soil erosion which is now one of Haiti's greatest problems. As forest is cut back for firewood and cultivation, the removal of the tree cover affects rain conditions and causes erosion, which leads to the abandonment of cleared plots and the establishment of new clearings, so repeating the cycle. Over the years this ecological devastation has intensified as population growth has increased the pressure on the land. The peasants, with their meagre resources, have been unable to invest in soil conservation.

The mainstays of the post-independence economy were coffee production and export, timber exports and smuggling. The break-up of the plantations hastened the transfer from sugar to coffee growing, which could be carried out on small hilly plots, for which sugar cane was unsuitable. The majority of the ex-slaves worked as subsistence farmers. In the towns, commercial and bureaucratic elites emerged who were French speaking, practised Christianity and operated a written culture. This excluded the rural peasantry from power, who spoke Creole, practised voodoo and possessed an oral culture. Although Dessalines had massacred the remaining French planters in 1805 and foreigners were constitutionally forbidden to own property in Haiti, the image of the 'useful' white person was retained in the shape of doctors, teachers and priests. The urban elites aspired to French styles of behaviour, establishing a social order based on skin colour. The conflict between the mulatto and black elites became a permanent source of political instability.

The main features of Haitian political behaviour were established at this time: an emphasis on personal power, reliance on armed force to hold power, and open financial corruption. The narrow social base of the new urban elite led to a search for legitimacy through the person of a powerful individual who could invent his own laws and ideology. A succession of presidents, kings and emperors fitting this specification culminated in its most characteristic manifestation: François Duvalier.

The incumbent's power, however, rested on armed force. The maintenance of a large military establishment was less necessary after the French had recognized Haitian independence. The collapse of the plantation system also ended the need for military economic discipline. Nevertheless, the army soon found a new role. Successive uprisings throughout the nineteenth century spawned a series of violent sabre-rattling and parade-ground generals. Since every armed revolt achieved its aims, however briefly, all kinds of adventurers were encouraged to cover themselves with decorations and bestow whatever rank they chose upon themselves; sometimes children were born with the rank of general.

At the same time, the economy needed capital. During the first twenty years, before independence was recognized, no foreign credit institution lent money to Haiti. The country had no banks; a banking system was not set up until 1880. The only source of capital was the public coffers, which tradition had already thrown open to private greed and ambition. Successive heads of government plundered them unscrupulously. 'Pluck the chicken,' Dessalines had urged, 'so long as it does not squawk.' Likewise, the majority of imports and exports bypassed any customs control. The tradition of arbitrary illegality in Haitian life was given a new boost.

With the fall of each successive government, it was discovered that the public treasury was empty, and the incoming government had to borrow heavily. The complete failure to invest in productive sectors of the economy meant that by the end of the nineteenth century, 80 per cent of revenue was going on debt repayments. European nations

Mark Edwards/Earthscan

Serious erosion in area previously mangrove forest

19

contributed to the plundering by regularly demanding compensation for allegedly maltreated subjects. As the fragile economic structure of the country crumbled away towards the end of the century, French and German businessmen began to invest in commerce and public utilities. This aroused some alarm in the United States, which had little investment in Haiti, but was taking an increasing share of Haitian trade and was also concerned about Haiti's strategic position. The US Assistant Secretary of State, Alvey Adee, had described the country in 1888 as 'a public nuisance at our doors.' In 1904 the Roosevelt Corollary to the Monroe Doctrine proclaimed that the inability of a Caribbean nation to pay its debts, where this might lead to European intervention, was cause for intervention by the US.

US occupation and after

In the latter part of the nineteenth century, the black-mulatto division had to some extent been kept in check by the *politique de doublure*. This arrangement meant that the mulattoes ran the country through their control of key government ministries, the bureaucratic apparatus and the commercial sector, behind a facade of black rule personified by a black president. As the nation's indebtedness increased, the growing financial chaos and the increasing impoverishment of the countryside put the system under severe strain. The unrest of the rural poor began to threaten the security of the elite, and no faction was strong enough to retain power for long. Between 1911 and 1915, seven Presidents were overthrown; the last of them was President Vilbrun Guillaume Sam, who was torn apart by an angry crowd in July 1915.

The United States used Sam's death as a pretext to occupy the country. It had a cruiser in Port-au-Prince waiting for just such an event, and in December 1914 a detachment of US Marines had seized the government's gold deposits from the Banque Nationale at gunpoint. The gold, valued at US$500,000, was deposited in the vaults of the National City Bank in New York, which was in dispute with the government over debt repayments and other financial matters. The July 1915 invasion heralded almost twenty years of occupation, ending in August 1934.

The United States disbanded the army, replacing it with a national *gendarmerie* under US officers. It established a customs receivership, effectively taking control of the national finances, and rewrote the constitution to permit foreign ownership of property. The US attitude to the Haitian political process was summed up by a message from Admiral William Caperton to the Navy Secretary in Washington, Joseph Daniels, in August 1915; 'Next Thursday, 12 August, unless

US occupation

The political and financial condition of Hayti is so deplorable that right-thinking men are brought to the conclusion that something must be done; that a great effort must be made to free their country, and that something can lie only in the direction of assistance from the United States, the logical guide and protector of all the Latin American republics. There is but one remedy for existing conditions, and that is the establishment of an honest and stable government, through and by the assistance of the United States. The good Haytians, the true patriots, having put aside all foolish national ambitions, realize that no other beneficial course can be pursued.

Haitian resident in New York, quoted in the *New York Times*, 1 January 1911

Evidence that there has been 'unlawful, indiscriminate killing' of Haitian natives by some of the American Marines stationed there during the American occupation of the past five years was revealed today when the Navy Department made public the report of Brigadier General George Barnett, former Commandant General of the Marine Corps, covering in detail the questions in Haiti from the time the Marines were landed in July 1915 to 30 June, 1920.

General Barnett states that of the 3,250 natives killed in the five and a half years of American occupation, more than half were killed in the repulse of an attack on Port-au-Prince and during the following operations . . . On 2 September, 1919, he wrote a confidential letter to Colonel John H. Russell, commanding the Marine forces in Haiti, bringing to the latter's attention evidence that 'practically indiscriminate killing of natives had gone on for some time,' and calling for a thorough investigation . . . 'I think,' General Barnett wrote to Colonel Russell, 'this is the most startling thing of its kind that has ever taken place in the Marine Corps, and I don't want anything of the kind to happen again.'

New York Times, 14 October 1920

otherwise directed, I will permit congress to elect a President.'

Initially welcomed by the urban elite, the Marines faced a severe test between 1918 and 1922, with the outbreak of a peasant uprising against the occupation. The leader of the resistance, Charlemagne Péralte, set up a provisional government in the north in 1919, but was captured and killed in October of the same year. The revolt took on sufficient proportions to make it necessary for the US to call in reinforcements, who put down the movement with considerable bloodshed, killing several thousand Haitians.

Economically, the occupation tied Haiti more firmly to the US, which already supplied 60 per cent of the country's imports in 1903. From US$3.8 million in 1915, imports from the US increased to US$15 million by the end of the First World War, and the US share of the Haitian market remained at about 75 per cent during the 1920s. Attempts at capital investment were less successful, since the tenacity of the Haitian pattern of land holding put obstacles in the way of establishing large commercial plantations. The Dominican Republic (also under US occupation), Puerto Rico, Cuba and Central America all offered more tempting investment prospects. Some plantations were nevertheless established on state lands occupied by squatters, who were evicted. The US also built roads using forced labour, and provided a certain level of public services.

Politically, the occupation elevated the mulatto elite into the top ranks of government. Although in the eyes of the Americans, mulattoes and blacks were all alike, the US officers, who were almost all southerners steeped in racism, found the mulattoes more acceptable on the basis that it was the natural prerogative of lighter-skinned people to rule. Driven from participation in political life, the new black urban middle class of doctors, lawyers and teachers developed the theory of *noirisme*, which emphasised Haiti's African links and reaffirmed voodoo as a key feature of Haitian culture. One of those involved in the *noiriste* movement was Francois Duvalier.

After the occupation

When the Marines departed in 1934, Haiti remained firmly in the US orbit. The national finances were still controlled by US officials, and the Banque Nationale remained a subsidiary of the US Export-Import Bank. The *gendarmerie*, renamed the National Guard and Haitian-officered, nevertheless remained faithful to Washington's desires. These were transmitted via the US ambassador to the mulatto elite which remained in office for another twelve years, until President Elie

Lescot was deposed by a military coup, following a student strike and mass demonstrations against the corruption of his regime.

The twelve years of stability for the oligarchy were obtained at a price — paid by the poor. A concession to Standard Fruit for banana production entailed the mass eviction of peasants from their smallholdings. The hungry and landless Haitians were driven to work on the sugar plantations of the Dominican Republic, whose rulers intervened openly in Haitian affairs to make sure that the flow of labour continued. Cuban and Dominican money was spent in Haitian election campaigns, and the main street of Port-au-Prince was renamed 'Avenue Trujillo' after the Dominican dictator. This coincided with a massacre organized by Trujillo of 20-30,000 Haitians in the Dominican Republic, an event about which President Sténio Vincent maintained a shameful silence. His successor, Lescot, was a close associate of Trujillo. Any domestic dissent during this period was repressed; opponents were jailed, tortured, murdered or 'disappeared.'

By 1946 popular discontent was rising because of economic hardship. During the Second World War there had been further evictions as land was turned over to the production of fibres and rubber for the US war effort. Shortages of food and imported goods had brought disastrous increases in the cost of living. The popular movement, fed by the post-war international surge in favour of democracy and social justice, was also influenced by the 'black power' ideas of the *noiristes*. In the face of such pressure the army supported the election as President of a black ex-teacher regarded as 'progressive', Dumarsais Estimé. Although supported by the left, one of Estimé's first acts was to ban Communist organizations. During his four years in power, Estimé paid off the US debt, introduced income tax and some social reforms and encouraged the formation of trade unions. Economic development gave his black supporters an opportunity for enrichment which they grasped eagerly. Discontent revived among the workers and students, coinciding with hostility from the mulattoes. When Estimé tried to amend the constitution to permit his re-election, he was deposed by Colonel Paul Magloire in May 1950.

Magloire's regime saw a return to the classic *politique de doublure*. He presented himself as the 'apostle of national unity,' promising to heal the racial and class divisions of the previous four years. In practice, he favoured the old mulatto elite, joined by a number of ambitious black politicians. Backed by the army, the Roman Catholic Church, the elite and the United States, Magloire encouraged foreign investment, introduced an economic development plan and set out to attract tourism. In 1952 Trujillo made an official visit to Haiti and in

January 1955, Magloire went to Washington. He told the US Congress, 'We believe that our destiny is closely linked to that of the great American democracy.' At a press conference he said: 'Since the decree against communism nine years ago no red infiltration has been noted. Basically the people of Haiti are immune to communism because the goods are well distributed among everybody.' Vice-President Nixon paid a return visit to Haiti a few months later.

Magloire's blatant corruption, coupled with a clumsy attempt to prolong his term of office, led to his downfall. In December 1956 he and his family went into exile, leaving the traditional empty coffers. Nine months of political chaos followed in which Haiti saw five provisional governments and a one-day civil war in which seventeen people died. By the time elections were held (on 22 September 1957), the two main candidates were Louis Déjoie, representing the mulatto elite, and François Duvalier, who had been a labour and health minister in Estimé's government but had been bitterly opposed to Magloire. Duvalier had built up support in the army, among the black middle class and the rural poor. His main rival for the support of the black urban poor, the demagogue Daniel Fignolé, had been exiled in June after nineteen days in office as President; his supporters in the slums of Port-au-Prince were massacred by the police.

Campaigning on a promise to continue the reforms of the Estimé government and presenting himself as a simple country doctor who wanted honest government and a fair deal for the poor, Duvalier won 679,884 votes to Déjoie's 266,992, with another candidate Clément Jumelle getting 9,980. It was Haiti's first election with universal adult suffrage and despite undoubted irregularities, it was a genuine victory for Duvalier. Although Déjoie won Port-au-Prince and a few other urban areas (notably Les Cayes and Jacmel in the south), the rural vote went overwhelmingly to Duvalier, his supporters taking all the Senate seats. Déjoie was left with just two seats in the Chamber of Deputies.

4 The Duvalier System

François Duvalier is the only ruler in Haitian history to have founded a dynasty. Set against the previous record of presidents assassinated, overthrown or forced into exile either before their term of office was up or because they tried to prolong the term, his achievement was all the more remarkable. At the time of his death in April 1971, few outside observers believed that his son Jean-Claude would last in power more than a few months; yet 'Baby Doc' is now in his fifteenth year as President, a longer record than that of his father. There are, however, considerable differences between present-day Duvalierism and the original version — an indication of the strength and adaptability of the regime which Papa Doc established in 1957. Even granted that the Duvalier system has for most of its life depended on the goodwill of the United States, it is evident that father and son have both shown considerable skill and ability in picking their way through the minefield of conflicting interests and power groups.

The early years

Duvalier assumed office on 22 October 1957 — the number 22 was for historic reasons, of prime psychic significance for the dictator. His first priority was survival. Having witnessed the overthrow of Estimé by Magloire, Duvalier was determined not to risk a similar fate. The early years of his rule were therefore dominated by his drive to neutralize the major possible sources of opposition: the army, the Roman Catholic church, the United States embassy, the business elite, political parties and trade unions. In the second stage, from the mid-1960s onwards, he was able to negotiate from strength, reaching an accommodation with certain of these groups which would allow them to pursue their sectional interests on the understanding that supreme power remained with Duvalier.

Within a year of taking office, Duvalier had forced Déjoie into exile and Jumelle into hiding; two of Jumelle's brothers were killed. Hooded men known as *cagoulards* led by Clément Barbot, the secret police chief, kidnapped, tortured and killed suspected opponents. When Déjoie supporters attempted a business strike in support of claims that the September election had been rigged, armed Duvalier supporters forced their shops open and looted them. The *cagoulards* ransacked opposition newspaper offices and, with the proclamation of a state of siege by the National Assembly in May 1958 giving the government emergency powers, Duvalier transformed them into the Tontons Macoutes; they exchanged their hoods for dark glasses.

The state of siege followed a bomb explosion at the end of April, and in July, Duvalier was seriously shaken by an invasion in which a handful of former army officers and US mercenaries seized the Casernes Dessalines, the main army barracks, behind the presidential palace. After this incident Duvalier created a palace guard under his personal control, stationed in the palace itself, and strengthened the Tontons Macoutes. He had already 'retired' the army chief of staff, General Antonio Kébreau, in March. Other old guard officers were subsequently replaced by younger men and the proportion of black officers was increased. In 1964 Duvalier declared: 'I have removed from the army its role of arbiter and balancing weight of national life, a role which made it swing from side to side according to its own interests.'

It was also necessary to bring under control the agency which had played the key role in neutralizing the army and the political groups: the Tontons Macoutes. The Macoutes' chief, Barbot, who effectively ran the country during Duvalier's serious illness in 1959, was arrested and jailed in 1960. After his release, he became involved in a plot against Duvalier and was killed by the militia in July 1963. This was just one of the many attempts at Duvalier's overthrow during the 1960s, several of which involved high-ranking officers and close associates of the President. As well as removing Barbot, Duvalier institutionalized the Tontons Macoutes by renaming them the Volontaires de la Securité Nationale (VSN) and making them accountable to the presidency.

Duvalier was equally ruthless in tackling other potential opposition. The trade unions were brought under control in December 1963, when the Union Intersyndicale d'Haiti and the Federation Haitienne des Syndicats Chrétiens were dissolved and their leaders arrested or forced into exile. The Université d'Haiti was closed and replaced by the government-controlled Université d'Etat. The powerful US embassy had to be wooed as well as threatened, so Duvalier started by inviting a US Marine Corps mission to train the Haitian army and by offering the US military bases or guided missile stations in Haiti. When the US began to hesitate about future aid to Haiti as a response to Duvalier's repressive measures, he baited Washington by flirting with the Communist bloc. When the Kennedy government sided with President Juan Bosch of the Dominican Republic in 1963 in his attempt to overthrow Duvalier, the latter called the US bluff and succeeded in getting Washington's ambassador, Raymond Thurston, removed. Also expelled was the 70-strong Marine training mission headed by Colonel Robert Heinl.

Duvalier had an even more prolonged struggle with the foreign clergy in the upper reaches of the Roman Catholic Church. Again, he opened with a conciliatory gesture — the inclusion of a young radical priest, Père Jean-Baptiste Georges, in the cabinet as education minister. In view of the Duvalierists' stated support for voodoo and their criticism of the Catholic Church as divisive and colonialist, the appointment was designed to allay the clergy's suspicions. But it also served as a token of support for Haitian priests, as distinct from the largely Breton group which dominated the hierarchy.

Between 1959 and 1964 the government mounted a series of attacks on the church hierarchy, involving the expulsion of several bishops and priests, including Archbishop François Poirier, a Breton. By 1966 the power of the Bretons had been broken, and Duvalier reached an agreement with the Vatican which saw Monsignor François Wolff Ligondé appointed as Archbishop of Port-au-Prince, the first Haitian to occupy the position. Haitians were also appointed to other bishoprics.

The conflict was of key importance for Duvalier, since it also affected educational policy. The *noiristes* around Duvalier had long seen the predominantly church-controlled educational system as a channel for preserving the privileged position of the mulatto elite, and the Haitianization of the church went together with a restructuring of the schools' admission policies and curricula to ensure that more black middle class students were enrolled. There was an attempt to introduce Creole as a language of instruction in primary schools, and Haitian themes were to be emphasised in the school courses. The aim was not so much to provide a universal education (in 1982 illiteracy stood at 63 per cent, according to official figures, the true figure being about 80 per cent), but to aid the renewal and preservation of the class from which Duvalier drew his support. The struggle with the church also served to strengthen the image Duvalier was projecting as defender of the nation and true inheritor of the mantle of Dessalines and Toussaint.

The Duvalierist 'revolution'

Although Duvalier and his supporters constantly referred to his government as 'revolutionary,' while the exiled opposition has often described it as 'fascist,' little political coherence emerges in the ideology of Duvalierism. Displaying the evasions and ambiguities of many supposedly revolutionary countries within the United States' sphere of interest, Duvalierism was essentially a black nationalist ideology with a radical rhetoric. Apart from the flirtation of the early 1960s, it was and still is firmly anti-communist. In 1966 Duvalier declared himself for the 'defence of Christian civilisation against atheist materialism and the ideological intolerance of a levelling and inhuman communism.' The ideology became mystical and highly personal, with Duvalier portrayed as the embodiment of Haiti. The 1964 constitution which made him President-for-Life also gave him such titles as Sublime Maquisard, Uncontestable Leader of the Revolution, Apostle of National Unity and Renovator of the Fatherland.

The extraordinary 'Catechism of the Revolution' published in 1964 contained a Duvalierist version of the Holy Trinity, stating that 'Dessalines, Toussaint, Christophe, Pétion and Estimé are five founders of the nation who are found within François Duvalier.' The five are then described as 'five distinct chiefs of state but who form only one and the same President in François Duvalier.' The 'Duvalierist extreme unction' is described as 'a sacrament instituted by the people's army, the civil militia and the Haitian people . . . to crush with grenades, mortars, mausers, bazookas, flame-throwers and other weapons', enemies of the state. There is even a Duvalierist Lord's Prayer: 'Our Doc who art in the National Palace for life, hallowed be Thy name by present and future generations. Thy will be done at Port-au-Prince and in the provinces. Give us this day our new Haiti and never forgive the trespasses of the anti-patriots who spit every day on our country . . .'

Behind the rhetoric, the achievements were minimal. The Duvalierist revolution curtailed the political pretensions of the mulatto elite but touched few of their economic interests. For all the talk of redistribution of the national wealth, the poor in the Haitian countryside and the urban slums of Port-au-Prince remained poor. When Duvalier came to power the economy was already in a state of stagnation with the agricultural sector devastated for lack of investment. The US aid boycott, which lasted from 1962 to 1966, brought further difficulties to this impoverished economy. The arrival of US transformation industries at the end of the decade created thousands of jobs but on highly exploitative terms, and with little

The state and the people

When European or North American newspaper reports
predicted the downfall of François Duvalier's government
on the grounds that it had done nothing for the people,
they manifested a misunderstanding of Haitian history.
The masses there have never had the expectation that
the state would do any good for them. The state comes
to confiscate, to tax, to prohibit or to imprison; consequently, the less seen of it the better. When the Haitian
proverb says, *'Apré bondié sé léta'* (after God comes the
state), it is not the goodness or the benevolence of God that
people have in mind; it is rather his remoteness, his
unpredictability and his power.

David Nicholls, *Haiti in Caribbean Context*, Macmillan,
1985

long-term benefit to the economy. Grandiose infrastructural projects
like the Péligre dam swallowed up vast sums without producing
benefits on the scale which had been promised.

Duvalier became President with the support of the black urban
middle class, the medium-sized peasant landowners and those
peasants dependent on them. His political achievement was to hold
the support of these groups and build it into a lasting force. The urban
middle class was rewarded with an increased role in the bureaucracy,
while the peasant landowners and their followers were brought into
the power structure and given new opportunities for authority and
enrichment.

For the first time since the US occupation, sectors of the peasantry
were called up into the army and given local power and rights. The
Tontons Macoutes (VSN) became a means of reinforcing the structure
of patronage exercised by peasant landowners. The latter traditionally
employed casual labour, gave loans or credit, and acted as middlemen
between farmers and urban traders, particularly in the coffee export
business. It was from this sector that many members of the VSN were
recruited, and the organization developed into a network covering the
entire country. In this way it provided Duvalier with information
about what was happening even in remote corners of the countryside
and gave the local VSN members a stake in the regime by increasing
their authority over the peasantry in their districts. Duvalier also built
up a support network among the *houngans* or voodoo priests, who

Papa and Baby Doc

had an intimate knowledge of village life.

Duvalier's other great success was in perfecting the system of arbitrary personal control over the nation's finances. The main instrument for enrichment of the Duvalier family was the Régie du Tabac, a body originally set up in 1948 to tax tobacco, cigarettes and matches, but which Duvalier turned into an unaccountable monster which taxed almost everything possible, without any obligation to reveal either its income or disbursements. As well as swelling the family fortune, the Régie was an invaluable channel for pay-offs and bribes. Banks, state firms and foundations and foreign aid institutions became private treasure chests which could be tapped to satisfy the President's needs. Business mafias grew up, organising state *borlettes* (lotteries), issuing false postage stamps and overseeing smuggling activities. At a local level, the Tontons Macoutes carried on the old tradition of extortion and expropriation.

Jean-Claude Duvalier

François Duvalier died on 21 April 1971, narrowly missing the 22nd. His coffin was guarded by 22 soldiers and 22 Tontons Macoutes. Only three months before, he had indicated that he wished to be succeeded by his 19-year-old son Jean-Claude, and the necessary alterations had been made to the constitution (which had stipulated 40 as the minimum age for the presidency). The choice was approved in January in a referendum, by 2,391,916 votes to one, and Jean-Claude was installed on 22 April. Two warships of the US navy stood offshore from Port-au-Prince during the transfer of power and the US ambassador, Clinton Knox, greeted the new President by calling for an increase in aid to Haiti.

Jean-Claude's inauguration ushered in a fierce power struggle between the old guard Duvalierists and 'modernizers.' Within the ruling family, the two groups were represented respectively by Jean-Claude's mother Simone, and by his eldest sister, Marie-Denise. Marie-Denise was married to Colonel Max Dominique, who had commanded the presidential guard before falling foul of Papa Doc and being sentenced to death but reprieved and temporarily exiled. Conflicts within the ruling circles have continued ceaselessly since, but in 1980 the balance was shifted when the young President defied his mother to marry Michèle Bennett, a member of the newer commercial mulatto elite. The marriage signified a fundamental change in the politics of Duvalierism as practised by Jean-Claude.

Michèle Bennett's father Ernest is a wealthy businessman whose interests include coffee and cocoa exports and the import of a range of

Father, Son and the United States

With only a few exceptions, Haiti has been unfortunate in her political leadership in recent years. This was inevitable in a country with an illiteracy rate of over 90 per cent. The highly emotional people, who have little but tribal rule and superstition to guide their thinking, have been notoriously susceptible to demagogic political appeal. The political leaders by and large have approached their tasks with the utmost cynicism.

New York Times, 23 June 1957

Dr Duvalier has made it known that as Haiti's next President he wants aid from abroad so as to straighten out the country's finances, combat poverty and modernize its defense. He looks especially to the United States for help . . . Dr Duvalier said he would ask the United States Government for a fiscal expert to help correct the financial mess. In many instances, he added, public finances have been regarded as private affairs.

New York Times, 29 September 1957

The United States has decided to try to shore up the Haitian Government on the assumption that its overthrow might plunge Haiti into complete chaos. In explaining and defending this decision, State Department officials said today that they were aware of shortcomings ascribed to the regime of François Duvalier. But they insisted that Dr Duvalier had given more stability to the impoverished nation than had any of his numerous predecessors in recent years.

The Government at Port-au-Prince is threatened from within by bankruptcy and from without by a 'Revolutionary Front' coalition based in Cuba . . .

Officials concede that Dr Duvalier — he was a country physician — has many faults. Nevertheless, they maintain that he is not a dictator of the same stripe as Generalissimo Trujillo . . . Dr Duvalier is believed here to be honest.

New York Times, 28 February 1959 ▶

It is the virtually unanimous view of Haitians and foreigners here that Dr François Duvalier now rules this Negro republic as an unchallenged dictator.

New York Times, 28 May 1961

The young Duvalier has improved the political atmosphere since his father's death on April 21, 1971. 'He's a serious young man who seems to be trying hard,' a politically independent Haitian said . . .

Although at least 150 political prisoners are still held in the Fort Dimanche prison, most have been there since the previous regime. 'Those who have gone to jail under Jean-Claude were all involved in some concrete anti-Government activity,' a foreign diplomat insisted. 'No one has been arrested for his ideas.'

The improvement in the political atmosphere here has enabled numerous United States and international assistance organizations to resume or step up their activities here. 'We now think our help has a chance of getting to the right people,' a foreign economist said.

New York Times, 2 June 1974

goods including cars; he is the national BMW agent. She was previously married to the son of Captain Alix Pasquet, who was killed in the July 1958 attack on the Casernes Dessalines. The marriage, which robbed Maman Simone of her official title as 'first lady' of Haiti, displeased not only old-guard *noiriste* followers of Papa Doc, but also liberal critics of the regime. Grégoire Eugène, publisher of the Social Christian paper, *Fraternité*, wrote: 'Are we not handing back to the right on a silver platter the political power we thought we had won in 1946?'

By shifting his power base from the black middle class to the mulatto business community of Port-au-Prince, Jean-Claude Duvalier has transformed his regime into a more ideologically orthodox dictatorship which runs on lines understood by the conservative politicians currently in charge of the United States. Wholly dependent on US economic aid and political goodwill, Duvalier found it necessary to appoint 'technocrat' economic ministers acceptable in

Washington. The process has been a complicated one, as the frequent cabinet sackings and minor policy changes indicate. Counter-attacks by the 'dinosaurs' (as the old guard are popularly known), have temporarily removed Jean-Claude's appointees, while the Bennetts have also intervened against those who have trespassed on their territory. One such case is that of Marc Bazin, a former World Bank official appointed finance minister in February 1982 and sacked after five months for taking his anti-corruption drive too seriously. Bazin had described Haiti as 'the most mismanaged country in the region,' saying that 36 per cent of state revenue was corruptly diverted by unnamed persons.

Similar pressures and contradictions have been evident in the area of human rights. A period of 'liberalization' opened in 1977 under pressure from President Carter, during which Creole radio stations and papers like *Le Petit Samedi Soir* began to voice criticisms of the government. The regime began to hit back in 1979, and in November 1980, three weeks after Ronald Reagan's presidential election victory, it launched a severe crackdown on its critics. Supervised by the Port-au-Prince police chief, Jean Valmé, more than 100 arrests were made, including almost all the country's leading journalists and independent politicians. The offices and studio of Radio Haiti-Inter were wrecked. Many of those arrested were deported. However, Valmé, whose growing power worried the Bennetts, was himself sacked the following May.

The 1980 crackdown was sparked off by outspoken criticism of the government over the fate of 100 shipwrecked 'boat people' in the Bahamas, which Grégoire Eugène called a 'national disgrace.' Since then, the continually widening gulf between the corrupt and luxurious lifestyle of the elite and the wretched conditions of the mass of the people has produced further tensions. Forty people died in food riots in May 1984, followed by further arrests in July and November. These were ordered by defence and interior minister Roger Lafontant, now regarded, along with Michèle Duvalier, as the real power in the country. The Catholic Church, whose lower clergy and some bishops have become increasingly restive in recent times, has emerged as one of the main targets of the new wave of repression. Sylvio Claude, leader of the Christian Democrat party formed in 1979, has been repeatedly arrested, imprisoned and driven into hiding.

As the country's economic condition deteriorates and discontent continues to increase, Duvalier's room for manoeuvre is shrinking. The change in his power base won him a breathing space in his relations with the United States and in the internal struggles of the ruling groups, but by identifying himself so clearly with the mulatto elite, Jean-Claude is running the risk of creating the conditions for a

Jean-Claude Duvalier, his mother Simone (right) and members of the Presidential Guard inside the cathedral, Port-au-Prince

more widespread and united opposition. In particular, he has risked losing the support of the *noiristes* and the key peasant landowners and Tonton Macoute activists. Although there are evident strains between the VSN, the army and the elite counter-insurgency Leopard brigade (which work to the President's advantage), it remains to be seen what support he could command if either the US or the business elite decided he was a liability — or if a serious opposition movement manifested itself.

The repressive apparatus

No one knows how many people were killed under François Duvalier, but estimates go as high as 50,000. He was no exception in using terror; Haitian governments have always done so. What was exceptional was the universal nature of the terror, and what caught the attention of the world media was that those arrested, exiled, tortured or killed included well known members of the elite and even members of the dictator's own entourage and family.

Under Jean-Claude Duvalier, widespread human rights violations have continued, but the repression has been more selective. Since 1977 the number of deaths has considerably diminished. Throughout the presidency of Jean-Claude, internal conflicts in government circles have been settled by dismissal and exile rather than by arrest and execution. Since 1977 no official executions have been recorded but disappearances and unofficial killings by the VSN still occur. The regime still makes widespread use of arbitrary arrest, imprisonment without proper trial, ill-treatment and torture.

Under the constitution promulgated on 27 August 1983, Jean-Claude Duvalier is not only President-for-Life and head of the armed forces, but has the right to designate his successor, who in turn becomes President-for-Life after ratification by referendum. There is a single-chamber legislature of 59 deputies which meets for three months of the year; for the other nine months the President is 'endowed with full powers to pass decrees having force of law.' The assembly has never initiated legislation, but only endorsed government decisions. The President personally appoints magistrates and judges. According to the constitution, though mostly ignored in practice, arrests can only be carried out with a written warrant (except for those *in flagrante delicto*), and those arrested must be brought before a judge within 48 hours.

The armed forces currently number about 7,000; of these, the navy and air force account for several hundred and the counter-insurgency Leopards for about 600. The presidential guard numbers about 800;

Torture: a victim's story

Ernst Benjamin, a member of the Christian Democrat party led by Sylvio Claude, was arrested in October 1980. This account of his treatment by the Service Détectif in the Casernes Dessalines was published by Amnesty International in March 1985:

'Colonel V took charge of the operation himself. When I was led before him he began to be abusive, shouting filthy remarks at me. Then he began to interrogate me about my electoral campaign . . .

'A torturer called G hit me eight times on my right ear with the palm of his hand and four times on my left ear. Blood was running from my ears when the Colonel ordered him to use a stick. I was then beaten with a stick by a second lieutenant. On the orders of the Colonel, G hit me continuously while I was standing up. He stopped when I was about to soil my trousers. I was led out of the torture room for a moment in order to tie the bottoms of my trousers with string so that the Colonel's interrogation and torture room would not get dirty.

'Once back in the room, the Colonel ordered the torturer to tie my body into a kind of ball shape by tying my feet and placing a stick behind my knees and at the top of my forearms. I was hit about 150 times with the stick and just as I had stopped shouting and was about to lose consciousness, I heard the Colonel shout "Enough".

'At this point blood was coming from my ears, my wrists were bleeding profusely, and my buttocks, which had swollen up to my waist, were bleeding slightly all over. That night of 16 October I felt I was dying. I spent two months and four days there, being interrogated under torture six times. I was beaten, given electric shocks, and made to stand to attention for prolonged periods. This last torture would make anyone confess like an automaton.

'On 20 December 1980 the physical torture ended when I was taken from the cell in the Casernes Dessalines and transferred to the National Penitentiary.'

Haiti Briefing, Amnesty International, March 1985

the remainder are ordinary army personnel. The Leopards were set up in 1971 and are armed and trained by the US. When called into action in Janu... ...ded on La Tortue island, ...ith regular army troops ...

The ... ...8 has been the Volont... ...ns Macoutes, an armed ... ...are trained by the armed ... ...ceive salaries and conseq... ...goods and crops. Curren... ...ormed personnel station... ...lus plain-clothes membe... ...former mayor of Port-au... ...tical prison, Fort Diman... ...ure. Government ministe...

The ... ...killings, jailings, torture ... ...y means of which politica... ...tions, the church and the... ...nder the changed conditions of recent years in which some independent press and political voices have been permitted at times, the VSN's activities have been somewhat more circumspect. However, organizations such as Amnesty International and the Inter-American Commission on Human Rights (a body established by the Organization of American States), have reported in detail on arbitrary arrests, beatings and killings by the VSN as recently as 1983.

Currently, the security forces concentrate on certain categories of people for arrest; they include political party leaders, journalists, trade union activists, church figures and community development workers. Contrary to the constitution, political detainees are normally held incommunicado for long periods and are routinely beaten or tortured. The principal torture centre is the Casernes Dessalines, headquarters of the Service Détectif, the civilian secret police. Those subsequently released who have given details of torture to Amnesty International include: Evans Paul, a radio journalist; Ernst Benjamin, Christian Democrat party member; Gérard Duclerville, lay preacher; and Yves Richard, secretary-general of the trade union federation, Centrale Autonome des Travailleurs Haitiens (CATH).

Prison conditions are appalling, with political detainees in the Casernes Dessalines held in damp, dark and filthy cells, often naked or with the minimum of clothing. No visits, reading materials, correspondence or communication with other prisoners are allowed. Poor diet and insanitary conditions lead to frequent intestinal illness.

Peter Marlow

Tontons Macoutes outside Presidential Palace, Port-au-Prince

The OAS Commission in 1979 published a list of 151 prisoners who died in Fort Dimanche from 1974 to 1976, of whom 77 died from tuberculosis and 22 from diarrhoea. However, Fort Dimanche is reportedly no longer used as a detention centre. Some political prisoners are held in the main prison, the Pénitencier National (National Penitentiary), where the regime is less harsh than in the Casernes Dessalines, solitary confinement being replaced by overcrowding.

A report on human rights violations published by Amnesty International in March 1985 was described by information minister Jean-Marie Chanoine as 'lies' which showed a 'total absence of objectivity.' He said that in Haiti there were 'no disappearances, no selective repression and no terror in the countryside.'

The partial relaxation allowed by Duvalier since 1977 has been a largely cosmetic exercise which has not extended to the point of permitting genuinely independent political organization. A government committee set up in 1983 to examine the 'possibility' of allowing political parties issued no report, and indeed showed no sign

39

of life. When legislative elections were held on 12 February 1984 under the new constitution approved by the National Assembly just before its dissolution in August 1983, the Christian Democrat and Social Christian parties were not allowed to present candidates. Although 307 candidates stood for 59 seats, all were government supporters, including the 'independents'; candidates were vetted before their nominations were accepted. The Social Christian leader Grégoire Eugène, in exile since December 1980, was denied a visa to return until after the election, and numerous irregularities were reported in the polling.

On 11 May 1984 Interior Minister Roger Lafontant issued a decree banning all political activity except that of the 'Jean-Claudist' party, until new legislation appeared. The decree is believed to have been a contributory factor in the riots which took place at the end of the month in Cap-Haitien and Gonaives, although the spark in the latter case was apparently the beating to death by police of a pregnant woman.

Those who have ventured to set up independent parties have suffered severe persecution. The most well-known case is that of Sylvio Claude, who founded the Parti Démocrate Chrétien Haitien (PDCH) in 1979, together with his daughter Marie-France, the party's vice-president. Claude had previously been arrested by the VSN, beaten and given electric shock treatment in the Casernes Dessalines and deported to Colombia, all without warrant, charge or court appearance. These events had followed his attempt to stand in the February 1979 legislative elections against Rosalie Adolphe.

Shortly after the PDCH was founded, Claude was arrested and eventually charged with 'subversive activities.' He was found not guilty in March 1980, but the authorities refused a court order for his release. He was freed after going on hunger strike and subsequently resisting an attempt to force him aboard a plane at François Duvalier international airport. Rearrested in October 1980, he and Marie-France were tried with several others in August 1981 and jailed for fifteen years each. The sentence was quashed by the appeal court, and in August 1982 they were tried again, this time receiving six years. Both trials were described by independent observers as failing to meet internationally recognized standards.

In September 1982 Duvalier granted Claude and his colleagues a full pardon, but they were only released into house arrest. Spells in hiding and further arrests followed, one of them after his other daughter, Jocelyne, was beaten to make her reveal his hiding-place. In July 1984 he went back into hiding; Marie-France is in exile. The government claimed in March 1985 that Claude was 'at liberty.'

Grégoire Eugène was detained briefly after he returned from exile in

1984, and his paper *Fraternité* was suppressed under another decree of Lafontant's suspending 'unauthorised' publications. The country's only independent human rights group, the Ligue Haitienne des Droits Humains, founded in 1978, has also come under severe pressure from the authorities. In November 1979 a meeting held by the League was broken up by Tontons Macoutes and 40 people were injured.

Early in 1985, two political moves were made in somewhat unexpected quarters. Clovis Désinor, who was Finance Minister under François Duvalier and at one time thought of as a possible successor to him, announced in February that he intended to form a party which would 'seek to defend the exercise of all fundamental freedoms, and to increase the participation of every citizen in political life and action.' Désinor, who made his announcement in a letter to the weekly *Le Petit Samedi Soir*, said the move would 'fulfil the patriotic and Christian wishes of clear-thinking people.'

A month later Louis Déjoie, son of the 1957 presidential candidate who opposed Duvalier, said in Puerto Rico that he wanted to return to Haiti to meet the President to discuss solutions to the country's problems. Déjoie, a millionaire who has lived in San Juan since 1961, said he would also seek the return of family property seized by the government when his father went into exile.

Ventures like Désinor's fall within the traditional Haitian concept of a political party, which is that of a group of electoral clients linked by personal relations and loosely grouped around individual political figures. The nineteenth century parties (the mainly black National Party and the mainly mulatto Liberals) originated in this way, and throughout their life showed little practical policy differences. More recent parties which attempted to break out of this system were the Mouvement Ouvrier et Paysan (MOP), set up in 1946 and forced into clandestinity by Duvalier in 1958, although he had himself been an MOP official in 1946; the Parti Socialiste Populaire (PSP), which existed from 1946 to 1954 as a grouping of mainly mulatto Marxist intellectuals; and a variety of Communist and left-wing parties in exile, of which the most important is the Parti Unifié des Communistes Haitiens (PUCH).

During the early years of the Duvalier regime, numerous landings, armed conspiracies and outbreaks of guerrilla activity took place; all were suppressed with extreme savagery. A revival of such activities has occurred in recent years, organized by a variety of groups. The abortive landing of January 1982 on La Tortue island was the work of right-wingers directed by Bernard Sansaricq, a Miami-based exile some of whose relatives were massacred by Duvalier in the 1960s. A more serious challenge has been posed by the Hector Riobé Brigade, whose first action in August 1982 included an attempted aerial bombing of the presidential ranch north of Port-au-Prince. The brigade is named after a young man who fought a three-day battle with the army and Tontons Macoutes in 1963, killing many of them before committing suicide. It has also claimed responsibility for several bomb explosions in Port-au-Prince on New Year's Day 1983, in which a number of people were killed. Five men were jailed in October 1984 in connection with explosions. Other planned landings during 1984 were pre-empted by arrests of those concerned in the United States and Guadeloupe.

By early 1985 pressure from Haiti's overseas aid donors had increased for President Duvalier to allow some liberalization of the political system. He responded by announcing on 22 April that he intended to appoint a prime minister and allow political parties to function. Details of the proposals were announced two months later, when the legislative assembly approved them. Political parties would have to recognize the President-for-Life as the 'supreme arbiter' who would 'guarantee the stability of national institutions.' Parties, which would be subject to authorisation by the interior minister, would not be allowed any religious or racial basis, a 'totalitarian' ideology or any foreign affiliations.

Elections will be held in 1987 with the participation of approved parties, and a prime minister will subsequently be appointed from the majority group in the assembly, with the duty to 'faithfully carry out the instructions and thoughts of the President.' The assembly will be able to reject a government proposal by simple majority, and deputies obtaining the support of a third of the assembly will be able to introduce motions.

Duvalier's April speech was followed by an announcement that 36 political prisoners were to be released, including five men who had been jailed earlier that month for nine years on charges of involvement in the 1983 bombings. The interior minister said that the release of the 36 meant that there were no longer any political prisoners in Haiti.

However, the liberalization theme had been marred by the shooting of two men, one of them an accountant in the state insurance office, who were reportedly caught in possession of political leaflets.

While the reforms may be a sufficient sop to satisfy those who had been urging Duvalier to clean up the regime's image, they are clearly a long way from a genuine democratization. There is no reason to suppose that it will be any great problem to arrange a Jean-Claudist victory in the 1987 elections. The new system is not designed to permit, let alone encourage, opposition, and politics will continue to take the form of manoeuvring round the President by a number of 'loyal' but mutually hostile factions.

5 The Economy

Haiti is the poorest country in the western hemisphere and one of the 25 poorest in the world. Its economy is marked by severe structural problems, and there is an extreme and widening gap between rich and poor. The Duvalier family's personal fortune is rumoured to amount to some US$400 million, while the annual Gross National Product per head stood in 1983 at US$315. In the countryside, where people live outside the cash economy on the edge of starvation, it is about US$50 per head. Indices such as illiteracy, infant mortality and expectation of life are the worst in the hemisphere. Prolonged drought conditions since the mid-1970s have increased the country's external dependence, with much of the population living on food aid.

Agriculture

The agricultural sector is in a disastrous condition. Although an estimated 70 per cent of the population work in agriculture, its contribution to GDP is only 32 per cent. The World Bank and USAID have estimated that 78 per cent of the rural population live at or below the 'absolute poverty level,' compared with 55 per cent of the urban population. The overwhelming majority of peasants work extremely small plots, using basic tools such as hoes and machetes. Average plot size is under half a hectare, and the average land holding is about three-quarters of a hectare. Many farmers work widely separated plots as a way of spreading the risks of production. However, the situation in the rural areas is much more diversified that any average figures can convey; the Haitian peasantry have had to develop a very wide variety of survival strategies.

More than 50 per cent of the rural population own their own properties, and a large number of peasants also farm land belonging

Philip Wolmuth

'Coumbite', communal field workers at Grand Anse weed a contoured field of soya, which helps prevent erosion, but is not as effective as terracing

44

to another owner, on the basis of *de moitié*, in which the landowner receives half their produce. A substantial minority of the rural population work either unpaid for members of their family or as paid wage labour. The number of large estates, although small, is increasing with the arrival of foreign-owned agri-business in Haiti. The state is the largest landowner.

The prevalence of a large number of small landholdings results from the break-up of the plantation system after independence, when both Christophe and Pétion distributed state land to the populace. Landholdings have been further sub-divided since then due to inheritance. Land tenure arrangements can be exceedingly complicated, with plots being leased or sublet on the basis of custom and oral agreement rather than written contract. Disputes over land rights are frequent.

The dense population of the country (over 500 per square mile) has increased the pressure on available land, According to estimates from international agencies, only about 29 per cent of the land is suitable for planting, but about 43 per cent is in fact cultivated, often under conditions of great difficulty. Many farmers cultivate two, three or four dispersed plots, a situation which enables them to plant different crops appropriate to differently sited plots, to spread weather and disease risks and use labour more efficiently according to the plots' local climate and growing season.

Land hunger has led to uncontrolled deforestation, despite laws restricting tree-felling since the 1820s. Once heavily forested, Haiti has lost all but a tiny fraction of its tree cover; in 1954 the proportion under forest was estimated at only 7 per cent. The decline has continued since then due to the search for land to cultivate and also for fuel, since wood and charcoal provide about 85 per cent of Haiti's energy needs. The deforestation, which amounts to an irreversible ecological catastrophe, has worsened the drought conditions over large parts of the country. The country's output of electric power is now threatened as land erosion has led to the silting up of the rivers supplying the Péligre and Saut Mathurine hydro-electric power plants.

The main cash crop is coffee, which produces approaching a quarter of all export earnings (US$51 million in 1983, out of a total of US$213 million). Almost 400,000 peasants are involved in coffee production, while its sales are handled by a complex network of middlemen, 'speculators' and export merchants. A prominent member of the latter group is Ernest Bennett, President Jean-Claude Duvalier's father-in-law. High export taxes and merchants' profits have reduced the yield to farmers from coffee growing, and many farmers have switched from coffee to other export crops.

Sugar is the second export crop, grown on about 45,000 hectares and processed by four industrial mills and about 1,000 artisan mills; output from the industrial mills in 1984 was about 46,000 tonnes. The country consumes two-thirds of domestic production and since 1977 has been a net importer of sugar. The sole railway in Haiti, which runs north of Port-au-Prince, carries sugar cane to the giant sugar mill owned by the Haitian-American Sugar Company (Hasco). Other export crops are mangoes, cocoa and essential oils. Both cocoa and essential oils, however, recorded a sharp decline in exports in the first half of 1984, and in March 1985 the government removed all taxes from essential oil exports.

Crops grown for domestic consumption notably include maize and rice. Maize production in 1984 was about 250,000 tonnes, grown by thousands of peasants on hillside plots. Rice production was about 120,000 tonnes, grown mainly on some 36,000 hectares of irrigated land in the Artibonite valley, but also on dryland plots, where the yield is about half that on irrigated land. Inadequate supplies of maize and rice have led to a growth in wheat imports, about 70 per cent of the 167,000 tonnes imported in 1984 coming from the US. Other crops grown for local consumption include beans, bananas and cassava. Food production has not kept pace with population growth, and the prolonged droughts of 1975-77 and 1982-83 have reduced output of many crops. About a quarter of the country's food is now imported.

Haiti is also heavily dependent on food aid. In 1984 some 48,000 tonnes of wheat were imported from the US under the PL480 food aid programme. Foreign assistance in 1982, from all official sources, amounted to about US$120 million, of which US$44 million came from the United States. This compares with a contribution from the Haitian treasury towards the 1984-85 development budget of US$26 million. The proportion of food aid in the overall aid effort is impossible to determine but in 1981, the US PL480 programme was budgeted at US$30.1 million. An aid agency report of 1982 indicated that 250,000 children were being fed daily, adding that in 1976 there were nearly 150 overseas aid agencies operating in Haiti — one for every 33,000 of the population.

Food aid has become essential for many poor urban dwellers in Haiti, and although it does not reach the rural areas as extensively as is sometimes claimed, it has created problems for the rural economy in certain areas. The distribution of free food, for instance, undercuts the precarious market for local produce to the point that it is not worthwhile for the peasants to grow crops at all. To this extent food aid actually exacerbates problems of poverty and dependence. The other perennial problem is corruption, which ensures that a great amount of the donated food ends up making handsome profits for street merchants. An example, just before Christmas 1984, was the sudden appearance of US-imported raisins on the streets of Port-au-Prince, selling for US$1 per pound. A reported 700 tons of raisins had been imported by USAID, in boxes marked 'Gift of the American people — food for peace', which found their way to street traders. Other items openly on sale, originally imported as food aid, included tinned meat, cooking oil, powdered milk and corn meal. USAID officials claimed that only 1 per cent of relief food went astray, but a representative of one religious group told an inquiring journalist, 'How long have you been in Haiti? You must know what goes on.'

An outbreak of African swine fever in 1981 was a further devastating blow to the peasant economy. Pork accounted for 50 per cent of Haiti's meat consumption at the time, but the pig was an important part of the household economy in a number of other ways. Some families, for instance, depended on killing a pig to finance the school term for their children. Following the outbreak of the disease, the country's entire pig population was killed under a US-supervized programme, with consequent losses to farmers for whom pigs represented a substantial investment. Compensation, available in principle, was not always forthcoming or adequate. The US Department of Agriculture declared Haiti free of the disease in September 1984, and repopulation with pigs imported from the US is under way. The main beneficiaries are likely to be US livestock exporters.

Industry

Over the past two decades rural poverty has driven hundreds of thousands of people to Port-au-Prince in search of food and work. The city's population has grown from around 250,000 in 1965 to an estimated one million or more in the early 1980s; (the actual figure, as is so frequently the case in Haiti, is difficult to obtain).

Taking advantage of the abundant supply of labour, about 240 mainly US-owned companies have set up assembly plants in the Port-au-Prince area since the early 1970s, employing around 60,000 people, mostly women. These companies, using imported materials and components and producing for export, enjoy very favourable investment conditions, including tax holidays of ten years in the urban area and fifteen years in the countryside and no restriction on profit repatriation.

In 1985 the minimum wage was US$3.00 a day, and trade union activity is virtually non-existent. The Centrale Autonome des Travailleurs Haitiens (CATH), formed in 1980, was swiftly rendered ineffective by the breaking of strikes and the arrest and deportation of its leaders.

The assembly industries are the fastest-growing sector of the economy, contributing 18 per cent to GDP and accounting for approximately half the country's exports. The garment industry employs between 17,000 and 20,000 people. Other significant industries in this sector are electronics, toys and sporting goods. Haiti is the world's largest producer of baseballs, exporting 15 million a year. These are produced by 1,000 women at the Rawlings Sporting Goods factory at a rate of 30-40 per head per day, for a wage of US$2.70 (in 1984). Rawlings, which has a contract for all the baseballs used by the US American and National leagues, admits that it would cost 'a fortune' to produce baseballs in the US itself. The plant manager of an electronics company, Argus Industries, said in 1982 that the 'trainability and reliability' of Haitian workers had enabled the company to produce electronic components to US military specifications for ten years.

The growth of the assembly industries has led the Haitian government more than once to project Haiti as the coming 'Taiwan of the Caribbean,' and as recently as 1982 a USAID report said that such a development was 'a real possibility.' However, the assembly sector has contributed only marginally to government revenue and the number of jobs it has created has been insignificant in relation to the extent of unemployment and poverty throughout the country.

Because of the low level of domestic demand for manufactured goods, traditional industry is of minor importance. Locally produced goods include cement and other building materials, household goods, shoes, cooking oil, pasta and other foodstuffs, beer, soft drinks, cigarettes, matches, flour, soap and detergents. Government and private monopolies (the government owns the only flour mill and cement factory), backed by high import duties, have resulted in high prices, erratic supply of goods and smuggling. Although the government closed the Dominican frontier to trade in November 1983, the supply of contraband goods from Haiti's cheaper neighbour continues. In February 1985 the government closed down Sodexol, a joint state and private sector monopoly producer of cooking oil. The closure decree said the company, which was US$20 million in debt, had suffered from gross mismanagement, fraud and tax evasion.

The mining sector, which once contributed substantial sums to export earnings and tax revenue, ceased to exist in 1983, when the US-owned Reynolds company closed its operation at Miragoane in the southern peninsula. Plans for gold mining and oil prospection remain unfulfilled. Further industrial expansion is problematic, because of persistent water and electricity shortages. A combination of drought

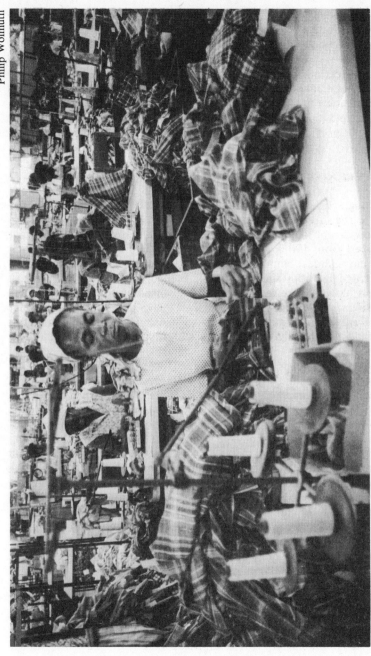

Philip Wolmuth

International Sewing Industries in the Free Enterprise Zone, Port-au-Prince. The 300 employees earn US\$28 per month (1983)

and silting up has cut power output from the Péligre plant in the Artibonite valley, which supplies Port-au-Prince; blackouts occurred for the second year running in April and May 1984. The assembly industries rely on their own generators as back-up. Transport and communications problems also hamper industrial development. Only 600 km out of the country's 3,000 km of roads are surfaced. Paved roads connect the capital with Gonaives and Cap Haitien in the north, and Jacmel and Les Cayes in the south. Port-au-Prince remains the principal port of entry, handling 90 per cent of the country's trade.

Tourism, commerce and trade

Although Haiti has at times recorded up to 275,000 stopover visitors a year plus a substantial cruise ship trade, the tourist industry today is at its lowest ebb since the mid-1960s. Arrivals are estimated to have dropped from 190,000 in 1980 to only 40,000 in 1983. Most hotels have been almost empty for the past two years, although certain self-contained facilities such as the Club Méditerranée are still able to attract tourists. The collapse has been caused by bad publicity about the 'boat people' and the blood disease AIDS, together with an image of poverty, corruption and repression which offsets the government's inefficient efforts to promote the country as an unspoiled tourist paradise.

When tourism was flourishing in the late 1970s, an associated sector grew up of itinerant vendors of paintings, carvings and other craft objects and souvenirs. The school of Haitian primitive painting became sufficiently fashionable for a number of entrepreneurs, mainly from the US, to open galleries and boutiques selling art works. The tourists also attracted large numbers of beggars, would-be guides and touts, as well as providing an income to taxi drivers, restaurant proprietors and stallholders in the Iron Market, one of the capital's principal tourist attractions. A large number of people will have had their earning opportunities reduced by the decline in tourism.

The commercial and business sector, concentrated in Port-au-Prince, is dominated by some 3,000 families who enjoy a standard of living, with an income of more than US$90,000 per year, which sets them apart from the mass of Haitians. The most profitable sectors are coffee and cocoa exports and the import of consumer goods. A community of 2,000 to 3,000 Christians of Levantine origin is prominent in retail and wholesale commerce, with younger members of the group now entering the professions. This community, whose first members arrived in Haiti in the 1880s, has tended to marry from within its own ranks. With rare exceptions they avoid any participation in Haitian political life. Retail market trading is almost entirely in the hands of black women, many of whom walk several miles from the countryside into Port-au-Prince, living and sleeping in the market area until their produce is sold. More prosperous market traders may also act as local coffee speculators.

Haiti's international trade is heavily in deficit, and strongly oriented towards the United States. The 1984 deficit was US$115 million, with imports of US$365 million outstripping exports of US$250 million. More than 65 per cent of imports come from the United States, and a further 10 per cent from other industrialized countries. Oil accounts for US$50-60 million. The US occupies an equally dominant role as a market for Haitian exports; the rapid growth of the assembly industry meant that manufactured goods, nearly all of which went to the US, accounted for more than half the country's exports in 1984. The US takes the majority of Haiti's exports, and the industrialized countries more than 90 per cent between them. The two most significant coffee markets are France and Italy.

Economic and financial policy

The overriding problem in Haitian financial life has traditionally been the lack of fiscal propriety. Generations of ministers and officials have been able to enrich themselves at public expense, while high earners have paid very little tax, and government revenue has depended on customs duties and indirect taxation. In recent years, international financial agencies headed by the IMF have been struggling to obtain reforms from the Duvalier government, threatening to withhold aid as leverage; partial successes have been scored.

According to World Bank figures, out of Haiti's estimated 6 million population, just 24,000 people own 40 per cent of the nation's wealth. One per cent of the population receives 44 per cent of national income but pay only 3.5 per cent in taxes. An IMF team which visited Port-au-Prince early in 1981 found that US$16 million had disappeared from various state bodies over the previous three months. They also found that President Duvalier had obtained US$20 million from government funds for his personal use in December 1980, and the central bank had been instructed to pay his wife Michèle a salary of US$100,000 a month.

A prolonged struggle took place in 1981 between the Duvaliers and the IMF over the terms of future assistance. The shortage of US dollars, which had circulated freely for nearly 60 years at a fixed rate of five gourdes to the dollar, led to the US currency being sold at a premium on the parallel market for the first time. Additional pressure was put on the regime by a Canadian government decision to pull out of a major rural development scheme because of 'technical and administrative problems and internal supervision difficulties' — a euphemism for the siphoning-off of funds. In October 1981 the new US ambassador, Ernest Preeg, criticized the regime for not having made a 'credible start' to economic reform. Similar criticism came from France and West Germany.

Duvalier conceded a point in March 1982 by appointing the former World Bank official, Marc Bazin, as finance minister. In his five months in the job, Bazin set about establishing accountability in the tax and banking system, separating the accounts of the central bank and the national bank of credit. He also imposed import quotas on a range of goods and started a campaign against smuggling and corruption. He was sacked in July and some of his measures were countermanded in a move engineered by Michèle Bennett Duvalier, whose younger brother Frantz had been jailed the month before in Puerto Rico for cocaine trafficking.

Bazin's successor, Frantz Merceron, has nevertheless continued to work along the lines demanded by the IMF. A 13-month standby agreement for US$37.2 million was signed with the IMF in August 1982 after the government agreed to implement a stabilization programme aimed at cutting treasury spending and raising revenue through fiscal reform. The Régie du Tabac, which was brought under the control of the central bank in 1982, was finally abolished in February 1985 and a new central tax department was set up; the Direction Générale des Impôts. Two out of three state projects criticized by the international committee of aid donors as a waste of public money — the Sodexol cooking oil company and a fisheries concern — were wound up. The third, a sugar mill at Léogane, has finally been opened.

Budget overspending in 1984 caused a failure to meet IMF targets and negotiations were still going on early in 1985. The 1985 budget, for the fiscal year starting in October 1984, totalled US$216 million, of which US$190 million was for recurrent, and US$26 million for capital expenditure. Debt servicing accounted for US$51.8 million. The ministries of the interior and defence, and armed forces and justice between them totalled US$31.1 million in recurrent spending, an increase of US$3.7 million. Eighty per cent of the recurrent budget goes on salaries. Tax increases so far have mainly been on consumer goods, with a rise in VAT from 7 to 10 per cent and additional duties imposed on fuel, cigarettes, alcoholic and soft drinks, cement and government services such as the issue of documents.

In January 1984 Haiti was designated a beneficiary country under

Key economic indicators

Income and prices

	1982	1983	1984	1985*
Cost of living index (base = 100 in 1982)	100	109	118	128
Change in cost of living index (per cent)	9	9	9	10
GDP at current market prices (US$ billion)	1.48	1.69	1.81	2.0
Rate of change in real GDP (per cent)	− 3.9	0.9	1.8	3.0

Balance of trade and payments (US$million)

	1982	1983	1984	1985*
Exports (f.o.b.)	197	213	250	280
Imports (c.i.f.)	− 334	− 352	− 365	− 390
Trade balance	− 137	− 139	− 115	− 110
Current account balance (includes service and transfer payments)	− 48	− 82	− 66	N/A
Overall balance	− 9	− 12	− 7.3	N/A
Change in net reserves (increase −)	17	29.8	21.8	N/A

Central government operations (US$million)

	1982	1983	1984	1985*
Treasury revenue	150	169	183	216
Treasury outlays	188	199	229	216
Treasury deficit	− 38	− 30	− 46	−
(in per cent of GDP)				
Treasury deficit	2.5	1.9	2.5	0
Overall public sector deficit	− 5.4	− 5.9	− 5.1	N/A

*All 1985 figures are US Embassy and Government of Haiti projections.
Sources: Institut Haitien de Statistique et d'Information, IMF.

Gross domestic product
(millions of gourdes, year ending 30 September)

	1980	1981	1982	1983
GDP (current prices)	7,229	7,422	7,378*	8,183*
GDP (1980 prices)	7,229	7,163	6,829	6,888
Percentage real growth	6.4	-1.0	-4.7	0.1
Real GDP per capita (gourdes)	1,443	1,404	1,313	1,307
Percentage real growth p.c.	4.5	-2.7	-6.5	-0.4

Source: International Financial Statistics.
*Estimate.

Sectoral origin of GDP
(1982 prices)

	1980		1983 (est)	
	US$million	%	US$million	%
Agriculture	539.3	32.4	525.8	32.2
Manufacturing	303.6	18.3	281.1	17.2
Mining	21.0	1.3	1.6	0.1
Construction	90.1	5.4	89.2	5.5
Commerce	295.8	17.8	294.8	18.1
Transport and communications	33.2	2.0	32.9	2.0
Electricity, gas and water	11.3	0.7	12.8	0.8
Finance	81.7	4.9	87.3	5.3
Government	160.2	9.6	173.4	10.6
Other services	126.8	7.6	134.0	8.2
Total	1,663.0	100.0	1,632.9	100.0

Source: IDB.

Main exports
(US$million)

	1979	1980	1981	1982	1983
Coffee	65.8	66.8	30.1	45.1	55.7
Bauxite	20.7	16.1	18.9	14.9	—
Sugar	3.5	4.9	0.9	1.8	1.5

Source: International Financial Statistics.

The national budget

Ministerial allocations in the recurrent budget for the 1984 and 1985 financial years (October-September) were as follows:

	1984	1985
	(millions of gourdes)	
Presidency	16.5	16.7
Legislative chamber	5.0	5.6
Finance and economic affairs	95.2	83.2
Agriculture	31.5	32.5
Public works	74.0	70.1
Foreign affairs	38.5	38.2
Education	94.8	96.3
Social affairs	16.8	16.8
Commerce and industry	15.8	13.9
Religion	3.4	3.9
Justice	12.2	18.5
Information/public relations	32.2	32.8
Interior/national defence	35.6	40.7
Public health	88.0	89.5
Armed forces	89.0	96.2
Mines/energy resources	6.9	6.9
Planning	20.6	22.7
Youth and sports	6.2	6.2
Total	682.2	691.1
Amortization of national debt		258.9
Sum total		950.0

G5 = US$1.

Source: Ministry of finance and national economy.

President Reagan's Caribbean Basin Initiative, allowing more than 3,000 items, with at least 35 per cent local content, to enter the US duty-free. The majority of the assembly industries currently operating in Haiti will not benefit from the measure, since they do not meet the 35 per cent local component criterion. The government and private sector are collaborating, however, on a US$2 million international industrial fair, to be held in Port-au-Prince in December 1985, aimed at attracting investment under the CBI.

The dollar shortage continued into 1985, partly fuelled by the rapid rise in the dollar against the peso in the neighbouring Dominican Republic. The premium being charged at the end of 1984 was about 8-12 per cent, a rate expected to remain more or less constant during 1985. The banking sector in Haiti is dominated by US, French and Canadian corporations. USAID has financed the creation of a development bank and a mortgage bank, which will give loans for industrial projects and residential housing.

The economic growth rate in 1984 was 2 per cent, following three years of decline or stagnation. The increase was attributed to the export assembly industry; domestic industry showed mixed results while agriculture remained depressed. Inflation was estimated at about 8-10 per cent. For 1985, US and Haitian projections show a growth rate of 3 per cent, inflation remaining at 10 per cent, and a trade deficit of US$110 million. The latest figure available for external public debt from the Inter-American Development Bank (IDB), for 1982, gives a total of US$535 million. The gross external debt was estimated at the end of 1983 as US$859 million.

Whatever the projections for the dynamic and externally-based sectors of the economy, the most severe problems will remain in the rural sector where three-quarters of the Haitian people still live.

6 Social Conditions

The urban elite in Port-au-Prince, including a reported 200 millionaires, live in luxury air-conditioned villas in the cool suburbs in the hills above the city, complete with tennis courts, swimming pools and carefully tended gardens, their needs met by a full complement of servants. Meanwhile, 90 per cent of the population live in conditions of destitution and squalor, their income failing even to meet the minimum wage of US$3.00 a day, without access to piped water, health care, adequate education or even food.

City and country

An English traveller at the turn of the century, Hesketh Prichard, wrote of his arrival in the capital: 'At first sight Port-au-Prince looks fair enough to be worth travelling 5,000 miles to see; once enter it, and your next impulse is to travel 5,000 miles to get away again', (*Where Black Rules White*, Nelson, 1910). Modern travellers have been known to react in the same way. Warning that 'it is necessary to walk through its cobbled streets with circumspection, for they are ankle-deep in refuse,' Prichard goes on: 'It is about the filthiest place in the world . . . No smallest effort is made at sanitation; the street drains with all their contaminations flow down and help to fill up the harbour. At times the rain flushes them, and this effort of Nature seems to be the sole force that tends to cleanliness.'

While the city centre is nowadays kept relatively free from such conditions, at least 200,000 people and perhaps many more live in the shanty towns set in a sea of foul slime which recall Prichard's description only too vividly. Baptised with picturesque names like Tokyo, Brooklyn, Nan Pelé, Bel Air and La Saline, the slums house 60,000 people per square kilometre, sleeping in three-hour shifts on

One of the luxury homes of the urban elite in the hills above Port-au-Prince

rag or straw beds in huts made of packing cases, boards and abandoned metal sheeting. Since refuse collection only takes place when a visiting dignitary passes by, rubbish piles up in the streets, making a mockery of public hygiene, but offering some comfort to the beggars and other starving people who rummage in it for dead animals, edible scraps or other pickings. Blockage of the drains by rubbish continues to cause unpleasant floods whenever there is heavy rain, one of the most memorable such occasions being on the day of President Jean-Claude Duvalier's wedding in 1980. A five-year IDB-funded drainage improvement and flood prevention scheme is now under way.

It is estimated that around half the city's population are without work and live below the poverty line. More than 10,000 homeless people sleep out on the streets at night. Concentration of wealth and employment in Port-au-Prince has worsened the split between the city and the rest of the country and accelerated rural under-development. The capital accounts for 40 per cent of GDP, 85 per cent of industrial value added, 90 per cent of industrial jobs, 98 per cent of energy consumption, 83 per cent of state expenditure, 85 per cent of medical services and 80 per cent of secondary education facilities. For the 75 per cent of the population living outside the capital, virtually no adequate services are available. The capital is often spoken of as a separate country, the 'Republic of Port-au-Prince.'

Health and education

Haiti's health situation is appalling. Infant mortality is estimated at 130 per 1,000, and increasing in the urban slums, while a third of all children die before the age of five. Some 40,000 children per year die, mainly from dehydration associated with diarrhoea; only three per cent of the rural population have access to piped water. The infant mortality rate in the US is 13, and in Cuba 14, per 1,000. Haiti's expectation of life is below 50. Tuberculosis, malaria and other diseases relating to inadequate nutrition and insanitary living conditions are widespread. An estimated 80 per cent of children under six have malaria.

The concentration of health facilities in Port-au-Prince means that in the rural areas, there is one doctor to an estimated 20,000 inhabitants and one dentist to every 100,000. Health care in the countryside is almost entirely left to international aid agencies. A 1979 report observed: 'Areas that fall outside of foreign-assisted programmes and that must be supplied solely by the Department of Public Health are under-supported and often neglected outright.' The government's spending on health in the 1985 budget is US$18 million, or US$3.44 per head of population for the year — almost all of which will be spent in Port-au-Prince. In the absence of much western-style medicine, treatment of illness in rural areas is often the work of voodoo priests or traditional practitioners using herbal remedies. The government has not sought to integrate traditional medicine into the national system.

Malnutrition is widespread, with a daily per capita calorie intake in the mid-1970s of 1,700, against a standard recommended minimum of

'Cité Brooklyn', Port-au-Prince

Flooding in Cité Simone

Peter Marlow

Family in the slums of 'Cité Brooklyn'

Axel Dupeux

*Three men pull 40 bags of charcoal for 20¢ (10 pence) per bag, Cité Simone
(1980)*

61

2,200. Droughts and crop failures since then have undoubtedly worsened the situation. In 1974, out of 129 developing countries, Haiti came 127th in calorie intake and 129th in protein consumption.

Education shows a similar picture to health provision. Although free and compulsory by law, the facilities are poor in rural areas (where only a quarter per cent of children are enrolled for school), and it is estimated that only 4 per cent of those starting school finish the primary stage. Obstacles to completion are cost (families have to pay for books and materials), and the alien nature of a school system modelled on the formal French system. French is the language of instruction, despite an unsuccessful attempt to introduce Creole, and school books are still imported from France. In the rural areas the nearest school may be out of reach; throughout the system classes are overcrowded and facilities inadequate. Government spending on education is slightly higher than that on health, at US$19.3 million for the 1985 fiscal year.

The state system provides some primary and secondary schooling, plus vocational, technical and university education; but private schools, mainly run by religious organizations, account for a significant proportion of secondary enrolment in the urban areas. The proportion of girl pupils is about a third for secondary schools and a quarter in further education. The educational system both reflects and reinforces existing patterns of class and cultural division in Haiti, favouring the children of the urban elite at the expense of the mass. The ultimate condemnation of the system is the illiteracy rate of around 80 per cent.

Women

Information about the position of women in Haiti is, not surprisingly, sparse. Women carry a disproportionate load of the work and suffering endured by the majority of Haitians. The evidence of infant and child mortality alone indicates the burden on women obliged to bear children doomed to die, with inadequate health facilities which endanger their own lives. Women also work on the peasant smallholdings and, under the widespread practice of *plaçage*, a male farmer may have a principal wife and one or more supplementary women working on dispersed plots.

In addition to working on the plots, peasant women are also mainly responsible for transport and marketing of produce. Some reports suggest that this tradition arose in the days when men travelling on country roads were liable to be press-ganged for military purposes or for forced labour. Women involved in marketing can gain a degree of financial independence, sometimes acting as local suppliers of loans and credits.

Religion

As in so many other respects, Haiti is divided in religion between the official Roman Catholic church and the popular voodoo religion. Following the prolonged dispute between François Duvalier and the Catholic hierarchy, the church remained acquiescent to the regime's will for some years, under the pliable Archbishop François Wolff Ligondé. Recently, however, Catholic priests and lay workers have again started to express concern about human rights violations and the overall condition of the country, encouraged by critical remarks made by the Pope when he visited Haiti in March 1983. Describing Haiti as blighted by 'division, injustice, excessive inequality, misery, hunger and fear,' the Pope called for a 'reawakening' of the Haitian church. 'Something has got to change here,' he said.

The speech was attacked by Ernest Bennett, Duvalier's father-in-law, and by the interior and defence minister Roger Lafontant, who said the government would never allow the church and its 'Marxist

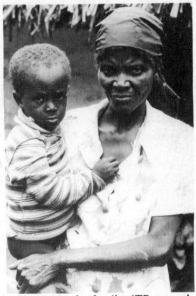

Philip Wolmuth

Women in production

Women in the family; 'TB corner', Jérémie

63

priests' to establish communism in Haiti. However, the government agreed during the Pope's visit to return to the Holy See the right to name bishops and archbishops, signing a document to this effect in October 1984. Under pressure from the rank and file, Ligondé was forced to support Catholic critics of the regime, and by early 1985, disaffection had reached the point where priests led a demonstration of 30,000 people in Port-au-Prince, shouting 'We have had enough misery.' Other demonstrations have been staged in the provinces. Church members were prominent among those arrested in the November 1984 round-up of 'subversives.'

There are also about 50 mainly US-financed evangelist Protestant sects in Port-au-Prince, which offer young people education, food and clothing. They have anything from 30 to 3,000 members apiece; recruitment is carried out by door-to-door visits or street evangelism, backed strongly by private radio stations. Insofar as these groups help to weaken the Catholic Church, the Duvaliers welcome them.

Voodoo, thought of by many outsiders either as a sinister rite or an artificial relic of the past kept alive for the amusement of tourists, plays an important part in Haitian life. Its roots are in West African religion, and since the days of slavery it has helped hold together a society created on the most fragmentary basis possible; slaves snatched from their homes and transported overseas with no rights at all as human beings. As the 1791 uprising showed, voodoo was a valuable channel for circulating secret information. In modern times, it operates as a system of social and cultural communication which is particularly valuable to the excluded masses of the population.

As a philosophical system, voodoo is based on the universality of the spirit, or the force of life immanent within all things, and towards which everything strives. This basis, which it shares with the animist religions of Africa, enables the spirit to be found in a tree, the earth, the sea or an ancestor. A voodoo participant who becomes possessed by a *loa* (god) has achieved communication with the spirit.

However, voodoo in Haiti has also absorbed symbols and ceremonies of the Roman Catholic church. As a religion, it operates both in private and public, with personal and communal worship. It is in the communal form that it displays the whole range of its religious characteristics: a hierarchy, ritual, liturgy and ceremonial forms.

Like any other religion, voodoo exercises strong social control, though it lacks the centralized structure and hierarchy of other religions. The priest or *houngan* is a person of importance in his community. When combined with the authority of the state, as in Papa Doc's time, he becomes extremely powerful. The successor regime, by turning away from Duvalier *père*'s identification with these village leaders, has put the task of control back in the traditional hands of the uniformed forces. Voodoo nevertheless remains as a basis for the outlook and attitudes of the peasantry, expressed in the multitude of Creole proverbs tending to emphasise acceptance, resignation and a certain cynicism towards the world at large. '*Déyé mòn, gin mòn,*' one proverb says. 'Behind the mountains, there are more mountains.' In other words, solve one problem and another one appears.

7 International Relations

As an independent French-speaking republic in the Caribbean, Haiti remained an anomaly throughout the nineteenth century. Uneasily sharing the same island with the Dominican Republic, it was isolated from the rest of the Caribbean, which remained under colonial rule. Its main economic links were with France and later Germany, but increasingly with the United States. Since 1915 Haiti has been firmly bound up with the US, politically and economically, although its dependence on the US has not precluded periods of tension and dispute between the two countries. The traditional isolation within the Caribbean has only recently been breached, with proposals that Haiti should be brought into the Caribbean Community (Caricom), which up to now has been composed entirely of English-speaking Commonwealth countries.

Haiti's principal contact with its neighbours and other countries further afield, however, has been through migration. The Haitian diaspora now reaches throughout the Caribbean as well as to North America and Europe, although it was the drama of the 'boat people' in 1980 which first made many outside the region aware of the extent of migration from Haiti.

Escaping from misery

Throughout the Caribbean, large numbers of people migrate in search of work and a better standard of living, either to other countries in the region or to the industrialized countries of Europe and North America. In the case of Haiti, there has also been an outward flow of political exiles; but the exodus of the boat people was a different phenomenon altogether, a spontaneous mass escape from starvation.

Migration in Haiti has been partly internal; some 50,000 people a year move from the countryside to Port-au-Prince, whose population increased from 250,000 in 1970 to 720,000 in 1982. Since only a minority of those arriving in the city succeed in finding work, the move means that the remaining thousands only exchange rural deprivation for the squalor of the urban slums. It is no wonder that the desperate Haitians seek another form of escape.

The numbers involved cannot be calculated with any accuracy, but some estimates say 1.5 million Haitians live out of the country. Up to 50,000 Haitians live, legally or illegally, in the Bahamas, working at the most menial jobs. Originally welcomed at a time of labour shortage in the 1960s, the continued arrival of the Haitians has led the Bahamas government to negotiate a treaty with Port-au-Prince giving it the power to return illegal immigrants. However, many children born to Haitian parents in the Bahamas are technically stateless; the treaty is expected to provide a means of regularizing their position.

There are several thousand Haitians in French Guiana, Guadeloupe and Martinique. Proposals have been made for the settlement of thousands more in Belize and Guyana. The largest numbers, however, are in the United States, Canada and the Dominican Republic. New York's Haitian community is estimated at 300,000, while the number of illegal Haitian immigrants in Florida is put by the US authorities at 25 to 30,000. A report from the International Labour Organisation (ILO) in June 1983 said that between 200,000 and 500,000 Haitians were believed to be in the Dominican Republic, of whom 19,000 were working on the state sugar plantations.

These 19,000 workers are recruited annually under a contract between the Haitian government and the Dominican Republic's state sugar enterprise, the Consejo Estatal de Azúcar (CEA). An ILO commission of inquiry which visited the two countries in January 1983 found that the recruits were kept in ignorance of the terms of the contract, and that if they tried to leave the workplace to which they had been assigned for the duration of the harvest (six to seven months), they were liable to be forcibly returned to it. Up to 1980 the workers had had one dollar a fortnight deducted from their wages and paid to the Haitian embassy for repayment on their return to Haiti; the commission found that workers had not received the deferred payments.

Since 1980, the system had changed. In addition to the cane-cutters' wages of 1.83 pesos per tonne cut, they were entitled to an incentive payment of 0.50 pesos, to be paid in a lump sum at the end of the season. The aim appeared to be to ensure that the Haitians did not desert the CEA estates for private estates where wages were higher; but in many cases there was a prolonged delay in making the deferred incentive payment. Evidence presented in 1982 to the UN Working

Group on Slavery by the London-based Anti-Slavery Society said that the wages were in any case 'miserably low' and that the working and living conditions of the Haitians did not come up to the standards laid down in the agreement between the Haitian and Dominican Republic governments.

In law, the Haitians have the right to join Dominican trade unions, and some have done so; but it is also widely believed that the 90 labour inspectors and 20 supervizors nominated by the Haitian embassy in Santo Domingo under the agreement include Tontons Macoutes, who keep the cane-cutters under surveillance for signs of trade union or political activity.

There have also been widespread and well-documented claims that illegal Haitian immigrants in the Dominican Republic are liable to be rounded up by the armed forces and taken to work on the sugar cane plantations. About 10,000 Haitians cross the border illegally every year, in addition to the Haitians permanently resident in the Republic, of whom an estimated 85,000 live on the plantations. An estimated 90 per cent of the cane-cutters in the Dominican Republic are Haitian.

It is not known to what extent the practices criticized in the ILO report have been modified since its publication in 1983; the Dominican authorities say that the deferred incentive system has been ended and have always denied the rounding-up of illegal immigrants.

There are a number of advantages in mass migration to the Haitian government. The departure of up to 50,000 people a year relieves some of the social pressures which might otherwise increase active expressions of discontent, while remittances from Haitians overseas contribute substantial amounts to the economy, estimated at anything from US$30 million to US$100 million a year. Against this has to be set the displeasure of governments which find themselves responsible for tens of thousands of destitute, illiterate and often diseased people washed up on their shores.

No one knows how many people have died in the leaky, overcrowded boats sailing to the Bahamas and Florida. Scenes of horror were commonplace in 1980 and 1981, including: the clubbing and teargassing by Bahamian police of 100 Haitians stranded on the islet of Cayo Lobos in November 1980, the drowning of 37 people within a few yards of the shore at Fort Lauderdale, and the murder of 90 boat people by two boat owners, both in October 1981. The Cayo Lobos incident in particular sparked off a wave of domestic criticism of the government, as journalists and opposition politicians accused it of presiding over a 'national disgrace' which had turned Haiti into an international pariah. The regime's only response was the round of arrests in November 1980 which ended the brief period of so-called 'liberalization.'

Up to 1,000 people a month continued to arrive in Florida until late 1981; but in September the Haitian governmment signed an agreement with the US permitting the latter to stop and return boat people, if necessary by armed force. Patrol vessels and aircraft were put into service in an operation costing US$1 million a month. Up to the end of 1984, a total of 3,107 Haitians had been returned to Haiti under the agreement.

While the then Interior and Defence Minister, Edouard Berrouet, praised the boat people for their 'courage' and 'enterprise' and promised to crack down on racketeers who took the migrants' passage money, the US authorities aroused anger by defining the travellers as 'economic refugees' ineligible for residence in the US. As thousands of Haitians were risking their lives to escape the misery of life in their own country, only to be turned back by the US government, the US was welcoming the Mariel exodus of 'undesirables' from Cuba. US officials described the Cuban exodus as 'stark evidence of the oppressive conditions under which Cubans live' and proof that the US was a 'strong symbol of freedom and a safe haven.' Only later did the US discover the problems they had brought on themselves with this application of double standards.

In principle, returned boat people are put into the care of the Red Cross and sent back to their villages of origin. However, there have been reports of returnees being arrested and beaten as *kamokins* or 'traitors.' The humiliation of seeing groups of people deposited on the dockside by the US navy aroused unusually strong nationalist reactions, not only in the opposition but reportedly among some government ministers. These critics from within had not complained in 1980 when Cap Haitien police fired on a departing boat, killing twenty refugees; at the victims' funeral, mourners had stoned the local police chief's car.

At the other end of the social scale, Haiti has suffered a steady exodus of doctors, teachers and other skilled workers. Some have left because of the higher salaries and better opportunities offered elsewhere, others out of despair or the need to escape political persecution. A high proportion of Haitian intellectuals live in exile: in Paris, New York or Montreal. Some estimates suggest that 85 per cent of Haitian professionals, technicians and other skilled workers are now living abroad. Five out of seven Haitian doctors live overseas, and it is said that there are more Haitian doctors in Montreal than in Haiti itself. The departure of such people is another link in the chain of deprivation which binds the Haitians who remain, ensuring that the country stays dependent on overseas aid workers to replace the emigrants.

Haiti and the United States

In a moment of enthusiasm after a round of talks in Washington in November 1981, the then foreign minister, Edouard Francisque, said: 'For the first time in history, we have the feeling that the United States will really cooperate with Haiti.' Saying that Secretary of State Alexander Haig 'understood Haiti,' he added: 'From now on we will work closely together. Haiti could be the Hong Kong, the Taiwan, the Singapore of the Caribbean.'

Delusions of grandeur are a constant temptation in the life of a politician, but on this occasion Francisque appeared to have strayed wide from the real issue, which was how far Haiti intended to cooperate with Washington. Although the US indicated that a 'redesigned' aid programme was in prospect, the Haitian government had to give something in return. First, agreement on the programme to intercept and return the boat people (who were costing the US a great deal of money as well as giving Washington a bad press), and secondly, cooperation with US plans for economic 'stabilisation.'

The US ambassador, Ernest Preeg, said at the time: 'The next two or three months will be decisive in instilling confidence here and overseas in Haiti's economic future.' Somewhat sourly, the French-language weekly *Information Caraibe*, published in Guadeloupe, commented: 'We cannot see how the Duvalier regime can manage to do in three months what it has failed to do in 25 years.' The subsequent prolonged wrangling over the IMF's demands for fiscal and economic reform seemed to prove the point. By early 1985, relations with Washington were once again at a low ebb; while Haitian government ministers were complaining of 'discrimination' against their country in the allocation of aid, US embassy officials were openly expressing impatience with the Haitians' arm-twisting techniques. The new ambassador, Clayton McManaway, was reportedly on extremely poor terms with interior minister Roger Lafontant.

A long standing US resident in Haiti remarked at this time: 'It is difficult to explain Reagan's love affair with this non-functioning place.' This may have been to overlook the way in which a love affair can take on the character of a power relationship. As long as the Duvaliers can present themselves as the only plausible upholders of US interests and the most effective barrier to communism, the US has no option but to continue supporting them. This was the basis on which Vice-President Nelson Rockefeller re-established normal relations after visiting Haiti in 1969, and it has been the foundation of US policy ever since. The principle was reaffirmed in 1982 by the House Foreign Affairs Committee, which after attacking the Port-au-

Prince government for corruption and incompetence, stated that the over-riding policy priority for the US was 'to maintain friendly relations with Duvalier's non-communist government.'

For the Haitian government, the principle that *'travay léta sé chwal papa degajé pa peché'* (looking after oneself in government service is no sin), has been easy to extend to relations with the US. The Duvaliers have become extremely skilled at using their nuisance value to extract financial support from Washington. In January 1985 Foreign Minister Jean-Robert Estimé used a ceremony in which he signed an agreement for a US$1 million development grant from West Germany to say that Haiti received 'insufficient aid' and suffered 'discrimination in the field of bilateral and multilateral cooperation.' He was generally understood to be criticizing the United States. An anonymous foreign diplomatic source commented:

> 'Duvalier is worried over the new austerity of Haiti's prime source of aid, the United States. Both the American State Department and Congress have expressed concern over the poorly functioning Haitian infrastructure, the seeming inability of Haiti's President to implement whatsoever the lofty ideals endlessly espoused in his speeches, the continuing suppression of freedom of speech, truly free elections, the muzzling of the internal press, and the unceasing graft and corruption permeating every facet of Haiti's public sector. Duvalier's constant assurances of the amelioration of these problems never seems to materialize in fact. Estimé's speech, praising West German aid, is a transparent attempt to play one of Haiti's supporters against another . . . Hunger and untold misery exists in Haiti, but Duvalier continues to speak of lofty and unfulfilled goals and never admits to any problems existing within his republic.'

Similar strictures were made known shortly afterwards to the interior and national defence minister, Roger Lafontant, when he paid his sixth visit to Washington in three months, together with Estimé. Discussions centred on US aid levels and were held with State Department officials and members of the Congressional black caucus, which had organized hearings on Haiti after the November 1984 round-up of alleged opposition activists. The two Haitian ministers were told that the US expected free elections, a free press and a genuine improvement in human rights observance before any aid increase could be considered. US aid for the fiscal year 1985 is US$34 million, against US$44.6 million for 1984 and US$43.5 million in 1983. It had been reported that the State Department was incensed by the Haitian government's 'arrogant' assumption that Washington's annual human rights certification was a formality. Nevertheless, in the complex web of political and administrative relationships in the US capital, there is no particular reason to suppose that the State Department's impatience with the Duvaliers will weigh that heavily against the traditional policy of support for the regime. The reforms promised by Duvalier in April 1985, backed as required by further gestures towards human rights observance will undoubtedly suffice to keep the aid flowing in.

The role of overseas aid

Foreign aid has essentially been concentrated in Port-au-Prince to support the assembly industry. Its most obvious results have been in the modernization of the city's basic services: road-building, street lighting, provision of a functioning telephone service, port containerization, sewerage and flood control. The paving of the main roads to Jacmel and Les Cayes, which has opened up the interior to integration with the economy of the capital, has been accompanied by large-scale purchases of land adjoining the highways by the Port-au-Prince oligarchies. This has given a further fillip to the rural exodus as the peasant owners are dispossessed.

In 1971, the first year of the 'development decade,' aid projects to the metropolitan region totalled US$167.3 million, against only US$45.2 million for the rest of the country. In fact, many schemes which should have been carried out in the interior have only ever existed on paper, and more especially on the payslips of those who are popularly known as 'payroll zombies.' Some schemes, like certain hydro-electric projects or the eradication of the pig population, have severely damaged the peasant economy to the benefit of the growing industrial and agri-business interests. In 1982 more than 200 Canadian missionaries in Haiti protested to the Canadian government over its support for a scheme to build two hydro-electric plants in the Artibonite valley, the country's most fertile region. The plans involved flooding 4,000 hectares and dispossessing 60,000 people to provide power for the Port-au-Prince industrial zone. The scheme now appears to have been dropped.

A USAID report in the same year stated that the final goal of its development aid was 'a historic change to a greater commercial interdependence with the USA.' An official commented that the 'transition' would be 'socially and politically delicate throughout this decade, especially for the rural sector, where 70 per cent of the population still live.' Recent aid decisions underline the emphasis on infrastructural development. In February 1985 the World Bank approved US$22 million in finance for electric energy projects, and the French aid agency approved a 15-year soft loan of 105 million francs for upgrading of the telephone system by a French company, CIT-Alcatel. France is also financing construction of a new runway at François Duvalier airport, to the tune of 84 million francs. (French exports to Haiti doubled to 181 million francs from 1982 to 1983.) Japan is providing US$2.3 million for hospital and medical care improvements.

About half the US government's assistance to Haiti is classed as development aid. PL480 food aid accounts for most of the remainder, and a smaller proportion is undifferentiated. In addition to food aid and the major infrastructural projects, a great range of smaller localized aid activity has been undertaken by non-governmental organizations from several countries. Many of these projects are founded on the principles of encouraging community participation and self-reliance; but in the authoritarian political environment of Haiti, an approach of this kind is not without problems, as is shown by the inclusion of a number of development workers among those arrested in the November 1984 roundup of alleged 'subversives.'

Caribbean neighbours

Haiti's long-standing isolation from its English-speaking Caribbean neighbours has proved hard to overcome. However, in July 1984, the Nassau conference of the Caribbean Community (Caricom) heads of government took a cautious step towards widening the organization's membership by allowing Haiti and the Dominican Republic to attend certain ministerial meetings as observers. The meetings concerned are those of the Community's health, education, agriculture and labour ministers. A technical committee was also set up at the end of 1984 to study cooperation between Haiti and Caricom in trade and foreign policy. Haiti also expressed an interest in establishing a 'strong association' with the Caribbean Development Bank. Since Caricom itself has recently experienced internal difficulties caused by the conflicting trade and financial policies pursued by some of its members, notably Guyana, Jamaica and Trinidad & Tobago, Haiti's observer status may have little practical significance. However, the decision is a political gain for the conservative Jamaican government of Prime Minister Edward Seaga, who made overtures to the Haitian government early in his administration in February 1981.

A preliminary visit to Port-au-Prince by Neville Gallimore, Jamaica's minister of state for Caribbean and Latin American affairs, produced a flood of rhetoric from the Haitians about the need for a

Caribbean front against 'international communist expansion.' The visit was returned by Michèle Bennett herself, together with the then Foreign Minister, Edouard Franciscque, and minister to the presidency, Henri Bayard. She returned with four pedigree goats, a gift from Gallimore, who is a goat breeder. Seaga subsequently mounted a prolonged campaign for Haitian admission to Caricom, which met a less than enthusiastic response from several other members, both because of Haiti's human rights record and because they feared the access of cheap Haitian goods to the protected Caricom market. The recent trade difficulties within the organization have only reinforced these anxieties.

The Dominican Republic

Haiti's most problematic relations, however, have been with the Dominican Republic next door. The two countries have rarely been on normal business-like terms, let alone amicable ones. At the peak of their revolutionary zeal, the Haitian slave armies occupied Santo Domingo. It did not return to Spanish sovereignty until 1809 and was occupied by Haiti again between 1822 and 1844. Echoing Toussaint l'Ouverture's words a generation before, President Jean-Pierre Boyer

Haitian cane cutters in the Dominican Republic work from 6am to 6pm on the Gulf + Western estate. The boy in the foreground is 13

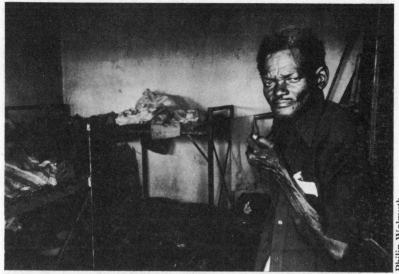

Living conditions for Haitian cane workers in the Dominican Republic have resulted in many older workers being close to starvation

in 1822 declared the island to be 'one and indivisible.'

The presence of Haitian troops, the imposition of Napoleonic law (particularly its effects on property ownership), and the post-1825 decision to increase taxes in the former Spanish colony to help pay Haiti's indemnity to France, all helped create an independence movement which eventually saw the birth of the Dominican Republic in 1844. Further attempts at reconquest by President Faustin Soulouque (later Emperor Faustin I) in 1849 and 1855-56 reinforced the legacy of hostility.

Subsequent key events in the relationship between the two republics were the 1937 massacre of Haitians, by which Trujillo established himself as the effective power in the whole island, and the brief conflict in 1963, when in the heady post-Trujillo days, President Juan Bosch concocted a plan to invade Haiti and overthrow Duvalier. Bosch had himself received information that Duvalier was planning his assassination, and was also provoked by a Haitian army incursion into the grounds of the Dominican embassy in Port-au-Prince, in search of a group of anti-Duvalier conspirators. He was unable to persuade his military commanders to take his plan seriously, however, and was overthrown shortly afterwards by General Elías Wessin y Wessin, the armoured corps commander.

For the rest of the 1960s and most of the 1970s, relations between the two countries remained frozen. President Joaquín Balaguer, who ruled the Dominican Republic from 1966 to 1978, observed a studiously correct policy towards Haiti. The border was closed in 1967, although subsequently reopened for the movement of contracted cane-cutters, and Balaguer sent a number of anti-Duvalier refugees back to Haiti. President Antonio Guzmán, the social democrat who succeeded Balaguer in 1978, broke new ground with a frontier meeting with Jean-Claude Duvalier in June 1979. The two met again at the end of the year to inaugurate a jointly-built dam on the Pedernales river. These meetings led to the reopening of the border for trade and helped to encourage economic cooperation. Bilateral trade nevertheless remained at a very low level, although smuggling swelled the total. With the Dominican Republic currently in a severe economic crisis (exemplified by the collapse of its currency), the frontier has again been closed since November 1983 in an attempt to reduce the volume of cheap Dominican goods being smuggled into Haiti due to the fall in the Dominican Republic's currency.

Despite their economic problems, many Dominicans still feel a mixture of superiority, contempt and fear where the Haitians are concerned. The more developed Dominican Republic not only has a higher standard of living than Haiti, but has succeeded in maintaining a democratic system of government since the overthrow of Trujillo and the subsequent civil war and US invasion. For the largely white or mulatto Dominican middle and upper classes, there is also a strong element of anti-black racism against the Haitians. The able and ambitious Secretary-General of the governing Partido Revolucionario Dominicano, José Francisco Peña Gómez, for example, is the subject of a whispering campaign which seeks to denigrate him because he is black and of Haitian origin. These differences in culture, language, politics and economic development will continue to present serious obstacles to the normalization of relationships. The present unequal relationship is symbolized by the lot of thousands of itinerant Haitian cane-cutters simultaneously valued by the state sugar corporation as virtual slave labour, and regarded by prosperous Dominicans with anxiety; the advance guard of a horde of hungry Haitians allegedly poised to pour over the border and plunder the Republic.

Haiti in the eyes of the world

It is not only in the Dominican Republic that Haiti is seen this way. Outside observers have, ever since Haitian independence, held a series of contradictory notions about the country's people. They are dignified and unspoiled, poor but happy, primitive and ignorant, oppressed and terrorized, kindly and gentle, lazy and incapable of running their own country, or brutal and depraved. Travellers like Hesketh Prichard sought to show that the Haitian example proved the impossibility of successful black government, just as property owners immediately after the slave revolt had argued that the Haitian experience showed the necessity for slavery. James Franklin, a British resident in independent Haiti, wrote in 1828:

> 'The system of labour so pursued in Hayti, instead of affording us a proof of what may be accomplished by it, is illustrative of the fact that it is by coercion, and coercion only, that any return can be expected from the employment of capital in the cultivation of the soil in our West India islands. I shall be able to shew that Hayti presents no instance in which the cultivation of the soil is successfully carried on without the application of force to constrain labour.'

In modern times, the plight of Haiti under the Duvaliers is often, albeit unconsciously, seen as in some way the fault of the Haitians. Even sympathetic observers have been known to ask why there is no effective opposition to the regime, or when a change can be expected; as if the survival of the Duvaliers is a mystery only to be explained by some deficiency in organization, energy or consciousness on the part of the Haitian people. The number of Haitians who have died, or who have been jailed, tortured or exiled for their opposition to the regime is one answer to that line of thinking. Another is to seek to understand the conditions in which Haiti came into existence and survived: its history and culture, the limits imposed on every Haitian's freedom to determine his or her own future by the country's position in the world system of power, and the crippling effects of its extreme poverty — much of which derives from historical and externally conditioned factors.

An interesting barometer of prevailing attitudes to a country is its tourist trade. In the mid-1960s, when Duvalier meant terror and the United States government felt he was a liability rather than an asset, Haiti's hotels were empty. As the Jean-Claudist 'development decade' got under way, the image changed; Haiti was being modernized and liberalized, and a tourist boom duly developed. The brochures described a country of 'incomparable splendour . . . unspoiled beaches . . . French and Creole *haute cuisine*, vibrant open-air bazaars . . . a fascinating blend of industrious and hospitable people.' The regime's success in internal pacification meant there was no street crime, and tourists managed not to see the squalor. At the premium end of the market, you could dine at the Oloffson, where in one

Haiti and racism

'A dangerous place of residence'

'The large majority, the pure blacks, descended from the former slaves, live in the interior in a state of deplorable moral and intellectual degradation . . . From their association with the French they retain only a blind and indiscriminating hatred of every white face; and this is the element that renders Hayti a dangerous place of residence . . .

'The wealthy Haytians derive their revenues from ground rents in the cities and the spoils of office; consequently they have little to lose by revolution, which is their occupation and amusement. By the black savages of the interior a revolution is always welcomed with fierce joy. It is their opportunity to loot and burn the stores of the hated whites. They are ever present in the imagination of the white residents as a fierce, irresponsible horde, ready at the first note of alarm to pour into the towns by thousands, and, maddened by rum, commit every imaginable excess.'

New York Times, 1 July 1888

'Racial weakness'

'The experience of Liberia and Haiti shows that the African race are devoid of any capacity for political organization and lack genius for government. Unquestionably there is in them an inherent tendency to revert to savagery and to cast aside the shackles of civilization which are irksome to their physical nature. Of course there are many exceptions to this racial weakness, but it is true of the mass, as we know from experience in this country. It is that which makes the negro problem practically unsolvable.'

Robert Lansing, US secretary of state, 30 January 1918
(*Lansing Papers*, Library of Congress)

evening you could spend the equivalent of a year's income for a Haitian peasant for the privilege of stepping into Graham Greeneland — as if Papa Doc had just been a character in fiction.

The current tourist slump, in which Haiti has fared worse than other Caribbean countries, reflects Haiti's image of the 1980s: the boat people, human rights violations and AIDS. Refugees had been sailing across to the Bahamas and Florida for more than a decade before the term 'boat people' was used in 1980. As early as 1968, the numbers arriving were sufficient to cause concern to the Bahamian and US governments. But it was the nightly televised scenes as the Haitians scrambled ashore which established the idea in the public mind. Likewise, it was the US administration's keenness to get value for their aid money that led it to highlight the human rights issue in Haiti, forcing the Haitian government to respond. Against this background, Haiti was in no position to counter the panic which broke out when Haitian immigrants were made responsible for the outbreak of AIDS in the United States.

Ironically, the high rate of disease and infant mortality in Haiti has meant that surviving Haitians are uncommonly rich in anti-bodies; hence the demand for Haitian blood, which once supported a thriving trade in blood to the United States. The trade was organized by the then interior minister, Luckner Cambronne. At different times an estimated 6,000 donors sold their blood at US$3.00 a litre, and five tons of blood a month were shipped to US laboratories run by companies such as Armour Pharmaceutical, Cutter Laboratories and Dow Chemical.

When allegations were made that AIDS, thought to have originated in Central Africa, was endemic in Haiti, the government reacted by ordering the closure of gay bars in Port-au-Prince and the expulsion of members of the US gay community. In August 1983 Health Minister Ary Bordes went to Washington for talks on the issue. But the image of AIDS as a 'Haitian disease' is hard to shake off, despite the statement in April 1985 by the US Centre for Disease Control in Atlanta that Haitian immigrants would no longer be classified as high AIDS risks because there was no medical justification for doing so.

Tourists might worry more that Haiti is no longer crime-free. In late 1984 and early 1985, an increasing number of armed robberies and killings took place in and around Port-au-Prince, including daylight raids on city centre business premises. US citizens were among those shot and injured. The police blamed migrants from the US, where they were said to have learned 'bad ways.'

The way that Haiti and Haitians are seen from abroad is affected not just by what happens in Haiti itself but also by changing perceptions outside the country. These are frequently influenced by developments in Haiti which are themselves the result of external factors. In short, to understand Haiti, look to the United States.

8 The Outlook

On 31 January, 1983, a son was born to the Duvaliers, named François Nicholas Jean-Claude II. The names suggest that there is no intention to cede dynastic power to an outsider. In a gesture to the twentieth century, Duvalier has retained the title President rather than adopting that of king or emperor, but in essence Haiti is governed by a royal family, and there is a Shakespearian touch to the palace intrigues surrounding the President-for-Life.

But Jean-Claude I is only 34 years old, and it would be a bold prediction to say that young François Nicholas Jean-Claude II is certain to inherit the throne. The fundamental lack of a true national politics in Haiti, denied by dominant minorities who have pursued their own fantasies and immediate desires at the expense of the nation, has handed the country over to the policy-makers in Washington. For want of a Haitian view of the future, it is the USA which applies its view of how Haiti should develop. A third Duvalier may not fit into the scheme at all.

It is even a moot question how long the current Duvalier will remain. The industrial and commercial development which has taken place since 1971 has created a substantial group of entrepreneurs who have an interest in efficient government. The ramshackle and corrupt Duvalier regime will have to accommodate to such people, as well as to their powerful backers in the US; but, since the whole basis of the Duvaliers' rule is personal aggrandizement and enrichment, they are unlikely to share the wealth and power without a fight. If the business class were to decide that the Duvaliers and Bennetts were an expensive and unnecessary luxury, and if they could construct a strong enough alliance of forces — which might require mobilizing and channelling the popular discontent — the Emperor might fall.

Washington has made it plain enough, in Grenada, Jamaica and elsewhere, that its preference is for conservative pro-business regimes which respect the norms of elected parliamentary government. Equally, it supports anti-communist minority undemocratic regimes in preference to unknown dangers, such as social upheaval and the possibility of revolutionary regimes or even radical nationalist regimes taking power. To a considerable extent, great survivors like the Duvaliers owe their continued hold on power to this ingrained fear of change on the part of the US. The dangerous moment for Jean-Claude will be if the pressure for change reaches the point where the US will have to accept it and decide which horse to back.

In 1979, Jean-Claude Duvalier said: 'I alone can blow the winds of liberalization. No one else can be put in power to blow the winds more strongly than I do. Never.'

Time alone will tell. But whatever the outcome of the next few years' power struggles in Port-au-Prince, the real problem will remain: the destitute millions of Haitians, for whom no one has any solutions, or offers any hope.

Further reading

Barry, Tom et al, *The Other Side of Paradise: Foreign Control in the Caribbean*, Grove Press, New York, 1984.

Bryan, Patrick E., *The Haitian Revolution and its Effects*, Heinemann CXC History, London, 1984.

Cole, Hubert, *Christophe, King of Haiti*, Viking Press, New York, 1970.

Diederich, Bernard, and Burt, Al, *Papa Doc: Haiti and its Dictator*, Bodley Head, London, 1969; Penguin, 1970.

Foster, C and Valdman, A, *Haiti Today and Tomorrow*, University Press of America, Lanham, 1984.

Franklin, James, *The Present State of Hayti*, London, 1828; reprinted by Negro University Press, Westport, Connecticut, 1970.

Greene, Graham, *The Comedians*, Bodley Head, London, 1966; Penguin, 1967.

Herskovits, Melville, *Life in a Haitian Valley*, Octagon Books, New York, 1964 (first published 1937).

James, C.L.R., *The Black Jacobins*, Allison & Busby, London, 1980 (first published 1938).

Lemoine, Maurice, *Bitter Sugar*, Zed Press, London, 1985.

Leyburn, James, *The Haitian People*, Greenwood Press, Westport, Connecticut, 1981.

Lundahl, Mats, *Peasants and Poverty: a Study of Haiti*, Croom Helm, London, 1979. *The Haitian Economy*, Croom Helm, London, 1983.

Mars, Jean Price, *Ainsi Parla l'Oncle*, Imprimerie de Compiègne, Paris, 1928.

New York Times, *The Great Contemporary Issues: Central America and the Caribbean*, Arno Press, New York, 1980.

Nicholls, David, *From Dessalines to Duvalier: Race, Colour and National Independence in Haiti*, Cambridge University Press, 1979. *Haiti in Caribbean Context*, Macmillan, Basingstoke, 1985.

Perusse, Roland, *Historical Dictionary of Haiti*, Scarecrow Press, Metuchen, New Jersey, 1977.

Prichard, Hesketh, *Where Black Rules White: a Journey Across and About Hayti*, Nelson, London, 1910.

Rotberg, R and Schmidt, Hans, *The US Occupation of Haiti 1915-1934*, Rutgers University Press, New Brunswick, New Jersey, 1971.

Roumain, Jacques, *Masters of the Dew*, Heinemann, London, 1978; first published 1944.

Weinstein, B, and Segal, A, *Haiti: Political Failures, Cultural Successes*, Praeger, New York, 1984.

Newspapers and periodicals

Le Petit Samedi Soir (weekly), B.P. 2035, Port-au-Prince.
L'Information (fortnightly), Port-au-Prince.
Haiti-Observateur (weekly), 50 Court Street, New York, NY 11201, USA.
Haiti-Progrès (weekly), 1280 Flatbush Avenue, New York, NY 11226, USA.
Caribbean Insight (monthly), 48 Albemarle Street, London W1.

Other LAB Publications

Paraguay: Power Game
September 1980. 76pp. £1.50

**Under the Eagle: US Intervention in Central America and
the Caribbean**
by Jenny Pearce
Updated edition April 1982. 295pp. £4.95

**The European Challenge: Europe's New
Role in Latin America**
June 1982. 244pp. £3.95

Brazil: State and Struggle
by Bernardo Kucinski
November 1982. 109pp. £2.50

Chile: The Pinochet Decade
by Jackie Roddick and Phil O'Brien
September 1983. 120pp. £3.50

The Poverty Brokers: The IMF and Latin America
October 1983. 130pp. £3.95

Guyana: Fraudulent Revolution
March 1984. 106pp. £3.50

Grenada: Whose Freedom?
by Fitzroy Ambursley and James Dunkerley
April 1984. 128pp. £3.50

Peru: Paths to Poverty
by Michael Reid
February 1985. 136pp. £3.50

Prices do not include postage